THE SPIRAL OF TIME SERIES

RAV DOVBER PINSON

THE MONTH of CHESHVAN

vol **8**

NAVIGATING TRANSITIONS
ELEVATING THE FALL

IYYUN PUBLISHING

Published by IYYUN Publishing
232 Bergen Street
Brooklyn, NY 11217

http:/www.iyyun.com

Iyyun Publishing books may be purchased for educational, business or sales promotional use. For information please contact: contact@IYYUN.com

Editor: Reb Matisyahu Brown

Developmental Editor: Reb Eden Pearlstein

Proofreading / Editing: Simcha Finkelstein

Cover and book design: RP Design and Development

Cover image: Cheshvan by Samantha Gray for Misaviv Calendar 5777
© 2015 De uteronomy Press, used with publisher's permission as a gift to the Iyyun Center.
See www.circlecalendar.com for more information.

pb ISBN 9781733813037

Pinson, DovBer 1971-
The Month of Cheshvan: Navigating Transitions, Elevating the Fall
1.Judaism 2. Jewish Spirituality 3. General Spirituality

vol **8**

THE MONTH
of CHESHVAN

NAVIGATING TRANSITIONS
ELEVATING THE FALL

IYYUN PUBLISHING

IN GRATITUDE

TO

REB MOSHE (MORRIS) & ARIELA WOLFSON שיחי'

FOR THEIR CONTINUED SUPPORT
AND FRIENDSHIP

זכות התורה חק' וסיועם תנן עליחם
ויזכו למלוא חפניים נחת מילדהם
מתוך בריאות ושמחה
ויצליחו מאד בכל עסקיחם
וימלא ה' כל משאלות לבם לטובה
מתוך אושר ועושר כל הימים

חון ועושר בביתו וצדקתו עומדת לעד

THE MONTH OF CHESHVAN

DEDICATION

LARA & CHESTON

MIZEL
שיחי'

in loving memory

of

שרה בת שרה
ע"ה

IN GRATITUDE
FOR THE SUPPORT OF:

GREG (GERSHON) & CHANIE BELL
& FAMILY

GENNADIY & SONYA BOGOLYUBOV
& FAMILY

JOEL KLEINER & FAMILY

CONTENTS

OPENING

*E*ACH MONTH OF THE YEAR RADIATES WITH A DISTINCT quality and provides unique opportunities for personal growth and spiritual illumination. Accordingly, each month has a slightly different climate and represents a particular stage in the 'story of the year' as expressed through the annual cycles of nature. The winter months call for practices and pursuits that are different than those of the summer months. Some months are filled with holidays and some have only one or none at all. Each month therefore has its own natural and spiritual signature.

According to the deeper levels of the Torah, each month's distinct qualities, opportunities and natural phenomena correspond to a certain set of coordinates arranged within a twelve-part symbolic structure. That is, the spiritual nature of each month is articulated according to its unique entries for each of the twelve categories:

1) a permutation of G-d's Four-Letter name 2) a verse from the Torah 3) a letter of the Aleph Beis 4) the name of the month itself 5) an experiential "sense" 6) a Zodiac sign 7) a tribe of Israel 8) a body part 9) an element 10) a unit of successive Torah portions that are read during the month 11) a season of the year 12) the holidays that occur during the month.

By reflecting on these twelve themes and categories, one reveals an ever-ascending spiral of insight, understanding, and practical action. Learning to navigate and harness the nature of change by consciously engaging with the cycles of time, adds a deeper sense of purpose and heightened presence to our lives.

The present volume will delve into the spiritual nature of the month of Cheshvan according to these twelve categories.

☾

NOTE: *For a more comprehensive treatment of this twelve-part system and the over-arching dynamics of the "story of the year," an in-depth introduction has been provided in Volume One of this series, The Spiral of Time: Unraveling the Yearly Cycle.*

Overview

The Month of Cheshvan:

Navigating Transitions, Elevating the Fall

CHESHVAN, FOR REASONS WE WILL CONTINUE TO EXPLORE, is considered a 'quiet' month. For one thing, there are no special days established for celebration or commemoration throughout the entire month. Due to this, one might think that it's a boring or spiritually dull month. However, from a deeper perspective, Cheshvan is actually an extremely interesting and empowering month. In fact, over the course of history many extraordinary events have occurred during this month that reveal its catalytic nature. But with regards to specific holidays, there are, and always will be, none during this time. Why?

Cheshvan is the first month (especially in the Land of Israel) in which one really feels the major seasonal changes that signal a shift from latent summer warmth to winter chill. When Cheshvan commences, the leaves are falling and the days are getting noticeably shorter, colder and rainier. This sudden transition, especially following the raucous intensity of Tishrei, can stimulate feelings of anxiety and uncertainty, as one is suddenly left all alone in a rapidly darkening world.

Tishrei, the *Sheva* / seventh month, is a month that is *Savuah* / saturated (with holidays) (*Medrash Rabbah,* Vayikra, 29:8). The intensive spiritual feasting of Tishrei 'fattens' us up and fills us with joy and inspiration in preparation for the oncoming cold, dark, wet, and lonely months of winter. It is therefore in Cheshvan, following the holidays of Tishrei and the preceding summer vacation time, that we 'come back to earth' and return again to our normal routine.

Accordingly, Cheshvan demands our utmost focus and attention in the moment, as there are no holidays in it to 'distract' us by pulling our awareness into some miraculous past or salvific future. In a month like Tishrei, when there is so much happening, we can get spiritually swept away, becoming so involved and absorbed in the happenings of the month that we forget about ourselves as it were. Because of all the external commotion we can easily lose focus on our own internal reality. But when Cheshvan comes around we are forced to focus inward, as there is nothing happening externally to distract us.

Accordingly, many people experience a desire to be alone during Cheshvan. This could perhaps be in response to the previous month of Tishrei when we spend days on end amid community and family. Additionally, as the world becomes colder and darker there arises a corresponding instinctual desire to retreat and recharge; all of nature is inclined to 'hibernate' or enter into their 'cocoon' of solitude during this time. Similarly, it was during this time that Noach / Noah entered the *Teivah* / Ark at the onset of the *Mabul* / Great Flood, which began in Cheshvan (*Bereishis* 7:11. *Rosh Hashanah*, 10b).

The flood story as a whole represents our experience during the winter months when people are prone to 'hide' indoors. When winter darkness approaches people tend to enter deep into their own arks, to 'hibernate' in a place of protection from the harsh elements, from the wintry 'angel of death' as it were. In fact, our sages tell us that Noach saw the Angel of Death approaching and so he hid in the Ark (*Zohar Chadash*, Bereishis, 68b).

Reflecting both the absence of holidays and the acute awareness of the days becoming shorter, wetter and colder, Cheshvan is also called *Mar Cheshvan* / Bitter Cheshvan. In many parts of the world, during this time we turn the clocks back an hour, which drives home the recognition that light is dwindling, and winter is about to begin. Simply put, this transitional season can cause people to feel down and bitter, making their surroundings seem gloomy or bitter as well.

Relatedly, the Torah tells us that following the wondrous Exodus from Egypt and the spiritual high of the Splitting of the Sea, the People of Israel were not able to drink the water "because they were *Marim* / bitter" (*Shemos* 15:23). The plain meaning of this verse is that they — the waters (a plural term in Hebrew) — were too bitter to drink. However, the same phrase can also mean that 'they' — the people — were too bitter. In other words, the people could not drink the water in the desert because of their own bitterness, since when you are bitter everything around you appears and tastes bitter as well (*Panim Yafos*, Shemos, 15:23). Just as the Israelites experienced a loss of energy and found themselves embittered on the heels of the miraculous revelation of G-d's presence in the Exodus, we too may experience a kind of existential 'hangover' in Cheshvan, as we come down from the spiritual 'highs' of Tishrei.

A SEASON FOR EVERY PURPOSE:

According to the sages, the year is divided up in a variety of meaningful ways. The simplest being a division into two halves, a warm half of the year, including spring and summer, and a cold/dark half, including fall and winter. In this construct, the six warmer months are considered more 'feminine' and are characterized by the quality of receptivity. Our corresponding spiritual practices during this time are more receptive in nature, since Divine flow is understood to be descending 'from Above to below' in this half of the year. The feminine nature of the warmer months is expressed in the presence of Hashem as a beloved friend, as it were. In this paradigm, Hashem is our loving parent, and we are Hashem's children. These months manifest the אור ישר / *Ohr Yashar* / direct light or illumination, as well as the energy of *Geulah* / redemption, which both emanate from Above. When nature is in full bloom we experience an enhanced sense of aliveness and an appreciation for the gift and bounty of life. In short, the Creator's blessings are manifest within creation in a revealed way during the warmer months.

The six colder months, on the other hand, are considered more 'masculine' and are characterized by the quality of giving (*Sha'ar HaKavanos*, Inyan Rosh Hashanah, Derush Aleph, Dalet. *Likutei Torah*, Vayetze. *Koheles Yaakov*, Yud Beis Chodesh. *Nahar Shalom*, 24a. Summer /Queen, *Pri Tzadik*, Teves, 16; Winter/King, *Ibid*, Tamuz 1). The masculine nature of these months is also expressed in the presence of Hashem as 'King,' starting with Rosh Hashanah when we anoint and crown Hashem as Cosmic Sovereign. From this perspective, Hashem is the King and we are Hashem's servants. Our spiritual practices in the winter are therefore more active, as we must elevate ourselves starting from 'below to Above.' In contrast to the 'strong and outstretched arm of Hashem' that we experience during Pesach and Shavuos in the spring and summer, during the colder/darker months we must work to redeem ourselves. This period is thus a manifestation of the אור חוזר / *Ohr Chozer* / reflective or returning light that we relay and give back to the Source. Any physical warmth experienced in these cold months is similarly self-generated or man-made; it is up to us to create it.*

More specifically, the year can be divided into quarters; two periods of three months within both the warm and cold halves of the year. Using this model, there is a parallel between the three spring months and the three months of the fall. In the spring, nature reawakens, the flowers start blooming, and the sun begins to shine brighter and for longer periods of time.

---

* Many Tzadikim would call these nights, which begins the colder and longer nights "The Holy Winter Nights" see *Seder Shana Achrona* (Munkatch), 104.

The spring begins with the month of Nisan, a month of miracles and redemption. The *Shefa* / Divine flow of life streams to us freely, and there is a feeling in the air of abundance and hope, freshness and renewal. Following Nisan is the month of Iyyar, a month of healing, and then comes the month of Sivan, the time of *Matan Torah* / revelation and giving of the Torah. All in all, the spring months express the quality of a gift descending from Above.

The months of the fall feel diametrically opposite. Coming out of the summer, the days suddenly begin to get colder, wetter and shorter. The sun shines with less intensity and heat, and even when it does shine, the daylight period is becoming shorter and shorter. During this time of year, the overwhelming sense is that the 'work' needs to come from below, from us. We need to create the heat, the light, the inspiration from within; or else we will remain cold and alone in the dark of winter.

The spring parallel to Cheshvan is the month of Iyyar. Neither Iyyar nor Cheshvan contain any real holidays. Although Iyyar does contain the 'unofficial' holiday of Lag b'Omer, and we do count the Omer throughout the entire month, meaning that a special blessing is recited on each of its days. In any case, the emphasis of both months is on self-generating and inner work. In Iyyar we work on our personality traits, especially those that determine how we present ourselves to the world around us and impact our ability to responsibly engage in interpersonal relationships. This is entirely appropriate for the warmer months that tend to bring us all into more social contact, as we are called out of our respective corners into the light of day, so to speak. In Cheshvan, however, the opposite occurs. As the summer fades, we instinctually begin to 'hibernate' or retreat deeper inward. We thus need to work on the more subtle aspects of the psyche that determine how we relate to ourselves such as self-starting, discipline, procrastination, and getting up after we have fallen down, as will be explored. These are the more *internal* issues that need to be dealt with during this season, as opposed to the more extroverted *Midos* / character attributes that we focus on refining during Iyyar in the spring.

In actuality, Cheshvan is really the second month of the fall season. But because the first month is Tishrei, which is saturated with the light and warmth of holy days, a vivid sensation of 'falling' into the inwardness and cold of autumn, is not truly felt until Cheshvan. In the "quiet" month of Cheshvan we register the natural world becoming rainier, darker and colder. As noted, after the physical highs of the summer and the spiritual highs of the holidays of Tishrei, many people experience a sharp emotional descent or a feeling of exhaustion or of being let down. If we surrender to this natural dip or drop in energy, Cheshvan can seem depressing — making it a fraught time of potential spiritual falling, as will be explored further.

However, despite this natural tendency of Cheshvan, the dynamic energy hidden within the month is the *Koach* / power to pick oneself up, to straighten oneself out, and to strengthen one's connection to the deepest truth. Through the spiritual work of Cheshvan, and then Kislev, we can gradually yet firmly root and elevate ourselves in order to generate radiant warmth and light from within. The fruition of this self-generative activity is revealed at the very end of the fall season, the culmination of Kislev in the holiday of Chanukah, the Festival of Lights.

The above is a general synopsis of the spiritual energies and processes at play in the month of Cheshvan. Now let us explore some specific ideas and practices connected to this month that will help you in your attempts to 'self-generate,' and to get up when you are falling or more firmly root yourself when you feel that you might fall.

☾

ᘐ

PERMUTATION OF HASHEM'S NAME

*T*HE FOUR-LETTER ESSENTIAL NAME, YUD-HEI-VAV-HEI (Hashem), is the Divine Source of all reality. The last three letters of the Name, Hei-Vav-Hei, create the word *Hoveh* / is. The root of this verb means 'to bring into being.' The first letter of the Name, Yud, serves as a prefix to the last three letters: *Yud-HoVeH*. In this way, the Yud modifies the verb to represent a perpetual activity (see Iyov, 1:5). The Divine Name can thus be understood to mean, 'That Which is Continuously Bringing Being into Being.'

For numerous reasons, the Essential Name cannot be spoken. Therefore a common practice is to rearrange its four letters into an alternate construction that may be pronounced as HaVaYaH, which literally means 'Being-ness.' This aspect of the Name refers to the Ultimate Being, which is the Source and Substance of all that is. The Ultimate Being does not depend on anything else to exist. It gives rise to all past, present and future manifestations, thereby bringing all things into existence ex nihilo, i.e., *Yesh meAyin* / something from nothing. Accordingly, the individual words for was / *Havah*, is / *Hoveh*, and will be / *Yihyeh*, are all encoded within the Essential Name Itself.

As the Source of all being and time, Hashem's Essential four-letter Name is intrinsically *connected* to actual time. For instance, each of the four seasons is connected to one of the four letters in the Name of Hashem. In terms of the months, this energy is expressed through a unique permutation of the four letters that comprise the Essential Name. Therefore, each month has an inner light that 'shines' through the 'prism' of a different permutation of the four letters of the Divine Name. Each permutation communicates a different spiritual dynamic which is part of the Divine signature encoded within that particular month.

The permutation of the four letter Divine Name corresponding to Cheshvan is the sequence Vav-Hei-Hei-Yud.*

---

* The vowels in the sequence of Hashem's name for the month of Cheshvan are Kubutz-Vav, Patach-Hei, Patach-Hei, and Sh'va-Yud. Although in this case the four consonant letters are derived from the last letters of the words in the verse of the month, the *Tikunei Zohar* [Hakdamah 2b] explains that we should always derive the vowels for each month's letter permutation from the first letters of the words in the selected verse.

To appreciate the significance of this particular permutation of the Divine Name, a basic understanding of the 'normal/natural' flow of letters will be helpful. The Divine Name is usually written in this order: Yud-Hei-Vav-Hei (י-ה-ו-ה). The letter Yud is in the shape of an elevated point, representing the Higher, 'masculine' giver, the Creator of all life. The shape of the letter Vav is similar to the letter Yud, only longer; instead of a singular point, the Vav is in the shape of a line, representing the Lower 'masculine' Giver, which is our own human potential of giving. The letter Hei in general represents the 'feminine' receiver.

The 'upper Hei' and the 'lower Hei' each succeed one of the masculine letters, meaning that they represent more 'hidden' realities or dormant potentials. The 'masculine' letters, Yud and Vav, precede each Hei, meaning that they represent more 'revealed' expressions and energies. In general, the 'masculine' letters initiate a process that is incubated or brought to fruition within the 'womb' or 'cauldron' of the feminine letters.

As human beings, we generally represent the receptive or 'feminine' paradigm; our potential is hidden within our depths, and we receive illumination and inspiration from a source above us (the Yud). However, in Cheshvan, our own innate potential to be a *Mashpia* / giver or initiator is more revealed and dominant. The letter Vav, which precedes the final receiver in the natural flow of the letters, is known as the 'lower Mashpia.' This represents the human being in relation to the Yud, which is the higher Mashpia, the Creator in the mode of 'the King of the Universe.' But in Cheshvan, this order is reversed; the Vav comes before the Yud. Not only that, but the Yud is actually the end of the energetic process initiated by the Vav. Our *Avodah* / work in Cheshvan thus begins with activating the Lower Mashpia, the human initiative and quality of giving and initiating action.

Here is the dynamic in greater detail: the lower Mashpia (the Vav), our own initiative, gives to the lower Mekabel (the lower Hei), our immediate life and surroundings, which is connected directly to the upper Mekabel (the upper Hei), our higher vision and values rooted in Torah. The upper Hei in turn, when activated, stimulates the Higher Mashpia (the Yud), the Divine Source. Since we do not, in this permutation and process, relate directly to the Yud — the Higher Giver or Hashem — the Yud is not openly revealed at the outset, but only becomes evident as a result of the process described in the order of the letters for this month. This conceal- ment of Divine Presence is reflected in the fact that there are no *Yamim Tovim* / holidays revealed in this month; in other words, there is no 'awakening from Above' in Cheshvan.

By contrast, if the sequence would have been Vav-Hei-Yud- Hei, our 'Vav' of human initiative would have again stimulated our Mekabel, the lower Hei. That however would have then awak- ened an arousal from Above in such a way that the Yud, by its own initiative, would reveal itself and give to the upper Hei. Thus propelling the process forward with an influx from 'above' so to speak. However, this is not the case in Cheshvan. The Yud remains 'aloof' and does not give from Above in the way of *Issarusa d'Le'ailah* / awakening from Above. In Cheshvan there is only an *Issarusa d'Le'tata* / awakening from below; meaning that any illumination or inspiration that we experience during this time is dependent on our own efforts.

Simply put, Cheshvan is all about self-generating, rooting, and raising oneself up, especially after a fall. We will continue to explore this theme below through various metaphors and corresponding seasonal phenomena.

ༀ

TORAH VERSE

T HERE IS A TORAH VERSE ASSOCIATED WITH EACH MONTH that is connected to its unique Divine signature, as explored above (*Tikunei Zohar*, Hakdamah 9b. *Eitz Chayim*, Sha'ar 44:7). The order of the letters in the Divine name for each month is an acronym for each month's particular verse (*Mishnas Chasidim*, Meseches Adar, 1:3). In addition to the order of the words and letters, the content meaning and greater context of the verse connected with each particular month is, of course, also part of the revelation of that month's guiding light.

The verse associated with the month of Cheshvan begins with the final word of a sentence: "…*U'Devash. HaYom HaZeh Yud-Hei-Vav-Hei…* / […the Land of milk] and honey. Hashem (commands you) today…" (*Devarim*, 26:15-16). *Devash* means honey, alluding to the power we have in this month to transform the *Mar* / bitterness and depression of Cheshvan, into sweetness and elevation.

Honey has a powerfully transformative nature; namely, whatever is placed in it becomes sweet like the honey itself (*Rabbeinu Yonah* on Berachos, 35. See *Rosh* ad loc). The power hidden within Cheshvan allows us to reverse its naturally 'bitter' taste (Mar), and elevate it to become *Ram* / exalted. This self-generated transformation turns Cheshvan into an uplifted (and uplifting) month of spiritual sweetness, as *Ram* is a reversal of the spelling of *Mar*. This represents getting up after a fall; or even better, using the momentum of a fall to catapult us deeper and higher towards the heart of our goal.

The four Hebrew words of this excerpted verse together have the numerical value of 416, or 16 x 26. The number 26 is the value of Hashem's Name, the Higher Mashpia. 416 is also the value of two times the name *Yitzchak* / Isaac (208). Yitzchak represents and embodies the quality of *Gevurah* / strength, and so two times the name Yitzchak indicates a double portion of Gevurah, hinting at the *Tikkun* / rectification for this month. It always takes Gevurah to straighten ourselves out and lift ourselves up in order to become a 'giver,' but it takes an additional measure of Gevurah to do so amid the *Din* / harshness, contraction, concealment and bitterness of having fallen from the onset. Sweetening one's situation or outlook takes strength and initiative, but to sweeten one's situation or outlook after it has become broken or embittered requires one to tap their deepest reserves of patience, perseverance, and passion.

Additionally, the value 416 is also the sum of *Noach* (58) and *Moshiach* (358). Noach and Moshiach, as we will see, are two main characters associated with this month, a fact whose significance will become more clear and meaningful in the following pages.

D'vash in this verse refers specifically to the honey from *Temarim* / dates (See *Rashi* on Shemos, 13:5). King David sings, in the book of *Tehilim* / Psalms, of a "צדיק כתמר יפרח / *Tzadik K'tamar Yifrach* / A Tzadik [who] will flourish like a date palm tree" (*Tehilim*, 92:13). The Baal Shem Tov teaches that this refers specifically to a Tzadik, a righteous and great spiritual person, who gives 'fruit' to others and inspires them (*Tzava'as Harivash*, p. 15b. *Baal Shem Tov*, Torah, Bamidbar, 3). This too hints at the Tikkun of Cheshvan — becoming a *Mashpia* / giver in order to uplift not only oneself, but others as well. Paradoxically, as we shall see, this goal of ultimate elevation requires one to go deep, immersing into the very realm(s) they seek to uplift.

The *Mabul* / Great Flood began and ended in the month of Cheshvan, and accordingly we read the Torah portion of Noach and the Mabul during this month. Noach, in the story of the Mabul, first introduced this Tikkun of helping oneself and others when they have fallen spiritually, mentally, emotionally, or even physically. However, according to the Zohar Noach only partially succeeded in this noble effort, as he really only extended himself enough to save himself and his own family; in fact many sages criticize him for. This is unlike Avraham, who prayed on behalf of the people of Sodom; and Moshe, who prayed on behalf of the people of Israel. We can see from this character development in the Torah a progressive expansion of the circumference of concern for others, which will ultimately culminate with Moshiach, who will uplift the entire world. To counteract our natural tendency to give only to our closest relations, we must train ourselves to actively care for others outside our immediate connections, especially those who have fallen or gone astray. We do this by straightening ourselves out, seeking to root ourselves ever deeper and picking ourselves back up again.

Even though, as Rashi maintains, our verse is referring specifically to date honey, when we think of honey in general, we usually think of bee's honey. And this is pertinent for the spiritual work of Cheshvan. Worker bees represent selfless giving and continually extending themselves in service to their queen and community. According to the Arizal, a person who was arrogant in his or her life may reincarnate as a bee, so that they can make a Tikkun by intensively learning to serve others (*Chesed l'Avraham*, 5:24). If you feel depressed, stuck in your head, sunk into a pit of problems, or on the verge of falling — the best way to strengthen yourself, regain your balance and start to rise up is to do something that actively and directly helps or serves others. Falling, standing, rooting and rising are all part of the meta-theme of this entire month, as will be explored.

☾

LETTER

There are twenty-two letters in the Aleph Beis. As the Torah, which is the 'Blueprint of Creation,' is written in Hebrew, the *Lashon haKodesh* / Holy Tongue, the Sages teach that each of these twenty-two letters contain a host of metaphysical energies and creative potentials. According to the Sefer Yetzirah, a profound book of early Kabbalah that pays particular attention to the inner dimensions of the Hebrew letters, the twenty-two letters of the Aleph-Beis are divided into three categories: three "Mother Letters," seven "Double Letters," and twelve "Simple Letters." Each month is connected to one of the twelve Simple Letters.*

---

*For a more in-depth analysis of all three categories of Hebrew letters and their relationship to the calendar, please see the introductory volume to this series: *The Spiral of Time: Unraveling the Yearly Cycle*.

The Hebrew letter associated with Cheshvan is Nun. The letter Nun has two different shapes: the common Nun (ב) and the
Final Nun (ן). The common Nun appears to have fallen and its
leg is collapsed, while the Final Nun stands up straight and strong.
According to our sages, Nun generally represents *Nefilah* / falling
(*Berachos*, 4b). This is not only because the word *Nofel* / fall begins
with the letter Nun — there are of course thousands of words that
begin with a Nun and have other meanings, many of which mean
quite the opposite, such as *Ner* / flame, or *Nes* / a raised flag. One
reason that Nun specifically represents *Nofel* is that it is a letter that
often 'falls away.' For example, *Lipol* means 'to fall,' but the Nun has
been dropped in this form. A more 'correct' form would be *Linpol*.
[The latter form is also used occasionally.]

Nun thus represents the idea of dropping away, or, in the case
of the 'final' Nun, of deepening in order to rise. During Cheshvan,
when we descend from the heights of Tishrei, our work is to stay
strong and learn how to bring the previous month's illumination
and inspiration all the way down into our lives. We thus transform
the energy of 'falling' or descending into 'flying' or progressing
through 'rooting' and grounding. In the words of Rebbe Tzadok of
Lublin, "Every month has something in particular that we have to
work on, and in Cheshvan our work is to strengthen ourselves and
get up if we have fallen down" (*Pri Tzadik*, Mar Cheshvan).

Nun also stands for the name *Noach*, whom we have already
introduced in relation to Cheshvan. In fact, we begin the month
of Cheshvan with the reading of the Torah portion of Noach. And
indeed, the Mabul / Great Flood actually began in the month of
Cheshvan, which is also the official beginning of the rainy season

in the Land of Israel. The other letter in Noach's name (נח) is the letter Ches, which is the number eight, alluding to Cheshvan, the eighth month of the year. [Cheshvan is the second month of the solar year after Tishrei, but the eighth month of the lunar cycle after Nisan.*]

The letter Nun in Noach's name alludes to the *Mabul* / Great Flood; in Aramaic, *Nun* means fish, implying that Noach was like a fish swimming and surviving in the turbulent waters of the Mabul. The story of Noach provides us with numerous hints and instructions for how to create the Tikkun of rising and rooting ourselves after we have fallen, awakening from below to turn our experience of *Mar* / bitterness into *Ram* / exaltedness.

We will now embark on an extended exploration of the story and symbolism of the letter Nun as expressed through the frames of Noach, the ark, the flood, water, rain, desire, relationship, prayer, survival, and salvation. As we will see, all of these themes play an important role in discerning the spiritual character and requisite work of the month of Cheshvan.

THE TIKKUN OF NOACH

The Mabul was a meeting and unification of the 'lower waters' and the 'higher waters.' As the Torah says, "All the springs of the great deep were split open, and the windows of the heavens opened up" (*Bereishis*, 7:11).

---

* Additionally, Menasheh, the 'tribe' of the month, offers his tribal offering "on the eighth day" of the Chanukas haMishkan, "On the eighth day, the Nasi was of the sons of Menasheh, Gamliel the son of Pedatzur" *Bamidbar*, 7:54.

In other words, while rain was descending from above, wellsprings opened up deep within the ocean and bubbled upward, 'flooding' the earth from both directions at once. The lower waters, which burst forth from underwater hot springs, allude to our task in this month of generating spiritual warmth from deep within the 'lower' realms (i.e. our lives and inner resources). Noach is, for this reason, credited with bridging the divide between the higher and lower worlds, and thus the Torah calls him a Tzadik. Nevertheless, as mentioned, this unification mainly benefited him and his own family, but did not bring healing to others, much less the entire world.

When the Torah tells us that Noach was a Tzadik, it immediately follows that he had three boys, "Noach was a Tzadik, *Tamim /* perfect in (relative to) his generation; Noach walked with Elokim… and Noach begat three sons…" (*Bereishis,* 6:9-10). From these verses, it appears as if it was due to the fact he had sons that the Torah calls him a Tzadik. Perhaps this is related to another teaching by our sages; the Gemara explains: אשה מזרעת תחילה יולדת זכר / *Isha Mazras Techilah, Yoledes Zachar /* When the woman releases seed first, the children born from this relationship will be male (*Niddah,* 31a). When applied to Noach and the above verse, which conflates his spiritual status with the birth of his three sons, this teaching from the Gemara alludes to the selfless generosity that Noach demonstrated in his relations with his wife. He was able to hold back his own desire, the release of the 'male waters,' to allow for the arousal of the 'female waters.' This intimate expression of selflessness and sensitivity was not enough to affect a Tikkun for the entire generation of the Mabul who, as we know, drowned in the Great Flood.

Yet it was enough to purify and save his immediate family and inner circle of intimates.

In contrast, the people who lived in the generation of the Flood are described by the sages as being obsessed with 'taking, to the extent of being thieves' (*Sanhedrin*, 108a). In other words, the pervasive desire of the generation of the Flood was to receive and receive, more and more. They had a one-track mind, with only one thought on repeat, 'give me, give to me' (*Mishlei*, 30:16). The *Tzidkus* / saintliness (or righteousness) of Noach was his willingness to reverse the natural desire to take, in order to consciously and compassionately give to another. In fact, he achieved this subversion of self to the extent that, he bridged the gap between the giving and receiving elements in the world, re-balancing the masculine and feminine qualities of Creation, thereby uniting the upper and lower waters. This practice and process corresponds to our *Avodah* / spiritual work during this month; when we initiate an 'arousal from below.'

According to the inner spiritual map of Creation, 'feminine' energies represent the lower waters, the role and function of the *Mekabel* / receiver. 'Masculine' energies represent the higher waters, the role and function of the *Mashpia* / giver ("המים העליונים זכרים והתחתונים נקבות / the higher waters are masculine, the lower waters are feminine" Yerushalmi, *Berachos*, 9:2).* Therefore, when we, like Noach, either give to others or work to uplift them, we stimulate and arouse the 'lower waters' — the recipient of our giving — to actively strive and flow upwards to merge with the 'higher waters.'

---

* Important Note: Feminine and masculine language in Kabbalistic and Chassidic thought is symbolic and energetically descriptive, not to be confused or rigidified into clear cut male/female gender distinctions.

On one level, the higher waters can be us when we are acting as a rectified giver, guide, or initiator. Ultimately they refer to the Source of All Life, the Highest Mashpia, Hashem. In either case, the result of such unifying action, as referenced in the verse above connecting Noach's spiritual status with his three sons, is the birth of righteous offspring (literally and metaphorically) who possess the capacity and inclination to give further. Thus continuing the life-affirming and uplifting spiritual process set in motion for the sake of Unification. In this way, we elicit a veritable 'rain' of blessings from the higher waters and the Ultimate Mashpia, Hashem.

We will deepen our exploration into the significance of rain and prayer in relation to Cheshvan within the following pages.

ESTABLISHING A FIRM FOUNDATION:
THE POWER OF YESOD AND THE PURPOSE OF THE TZADIK

"צדיק יסוד עולם / *Tzadik Yesod Olam* / a Tzadik is the foundation of the world," states the Book of *Mishlei* / Proverbs (10:25). *Yesod* / foundation is also the quality of active unification and connection, both energetically (or spiritually) and relationally (or physically). Noach was the Tzadik of his generation and thus had a great power to make a Tikkun and reconnect what was disconnected throughout the world. He had the power to heal and bridge the gap that had grown between the Mekabel and Mashpia; namely that the Mekabel must come to understand that although its main function is to receive, at times, it too can and must give. Kabbalistically, this is implied in the shape and character of the final Nun, representing a rectified Yesod and Yosef haTzadik, which bridges the divide and effects the *Yichud* / unity between the masculine energy of ZA (the six sefiros of Chesed - Yesod) and the feminine energy of Malchus (*Zohar Chadash*, Yisro, 45a).

Tamim, which can mean simple, whole, or complete, is another description of Noach. In fact, Tamim is a term used to refer to someone with a *Bris* / circumcision, as it says regarding Avraham who circumcised himself later in life, "and you *will be* Tamim." Noach was actually born *Mahul* / circumcised (*Zohar*, Bereishis). When Noach was born, his father named him Noach, "And he called his name Noach, saying, 'This one will comfort us in our work, and in the toil of our hands, that comes from the ground which Hashem has cursed'" (*Bereishis*, 5:29). What is the comfort that Noach brings? "He will bring *Nechamah*" says Rashi, based on the Medrash that connects Noach's birth with the historical introduction of agricultural technologies such as the plow, scythe, hoe, and other tools to work the land.

Before Noach came, humanity did not have things like plowshares. People thus benefited greatly by using these tools rather than their bare hands for the hard labor of working the land. Also it says, in earlier times when people sowed wheat, thorns and thistles would grow instead. This was due to the curse of Adam. But in Noach's time this curse subsided (*Rashi*, Bereishis, 5:29. *Tanchumah*, Bereishis, 11).

How did Lemech, Noach's father, know this would occur with the birth of his son? Perhaps he was a prophet (as the *Even Ezra* writes), or perhaps he merely hoped and prayed that his son would grow up to be that person to bring such comfort to the world (as the *Seforno* writes).

Adam once asked Hashem, following the episode in the Garden, "This curse of the land, how long will it last?" Hashem replied, 'When a child is born *Mahul* / circumcised, it will be a sign that this child that will bring Nechamah' (*Tanchumah*, Bereishis, 11). Noach was born Mahul, 'perfect' or Tamim, and thus heralded the dawn of a new age.

This quality of being Tamim also corresponds to the rectified 'masculine' (giving) energy and Sefira of Yesod. The Torah says that Noach "walked with Elokim." The Divine name *Elokim* corresponds to the 'feminine' (receiving) energy and Sefira of Malchus. When Yesod 'walks' with Malchus, it means there is a complete unity between the cosmic masculine or 'giver' with the cosmic feminine or 'receiver.' The Generation of the Flood caused a harsh separation between these Sefiros, whereas Noach lived in a way that harmonized and unified them, at least on some level, enough to save him and his family.

THE MULTI-DIMENSIONAL MEANING OF NOACH'S ARK

As an embodied microcosm of this cosmic dynamic, Noach activated the reconnection of Yesod and Malchus by entering the *Teivah* / Ark. The Teivah was 300 Amos long, 50 Amos wide, and 30 Amos high. [Amah is an ancient Near-Eastern measurement utilized in the Torah.] These dimensions add up to 380, the same numerical value of the Divine Names Shad-dai (314) and Ado-nai

(65), plus one for the *Kolel* (1) / the singularity of the word itself (*Zohar*, Parshas Noach). The Name Shad-dai corresponds to the Sefi-ra of Yesod, and the Name Ado-nai corresponds to Malchus. By entering the Teivah, Noach therefore re-connected and re-unified these names and their cosmic influence to produce abundance on both physical and spiritual levels.

The Arizal further explains how the dimensions of the Ark express its unique function as being the place within which the cosmic rebalancing of Giver and Receiver occurs. The Upper half of the Divine Name, Yud-Hei, represents the Giver. The lower half of the Divine Name, Vav-Hei, represents the Receiver. Yud (10) x Hei (5) = 50; the width in Amos of the Teivah. The Vav connects the upper Hei and the lower Hei. When the Vav is connected to the upper Hei, which, after being multiplied by the Yud (10), is now 50, it becomes 300. Vav (6) x Yud-Hei (50) = 300; the length of the Teiva. Of course, the Vav is also connected to the lower Hei. Vav (6) x Hei (5) = 30; the height of the Teivah. Thus, numerically, lettristically, and dimensionally, the Teiva is a perfectly balanced interweaving of Mashpia and Mekabel.

From another viewpoint, the Teiva is *Havaya* (The Essential Four-Letter Name) multiplied by *Ado-nai*. As illustrated in the chart below, when one places the name *Havayah* above the name *Ad-nai*, and multiplies the value of each letter by the letter beneath it, one arrives at the dimensions of the Ark. Yud is above Alef: 10 x 1 = 10. Hei is above Daled: 5 x 4 = 20. Together these products equal 30 (the height of the Teivah). Vav is above Nun: 6 x 50 = 300 (the length of the Teivah). Hei is above Yud: 5 x 10 = 50 (the width of the Teivah).

ה (5)	ו (6)	ה (5)	י (10)
י (10)	נ (50)	ד (4)	א (1)
= 50 / width	= 300 / height	20 = (10 + 20 = 30) / width	10 = (add to the product to the left)

THE WORLD OF, AND AS, RELATIONSHIP

Rashi writes that the cause of the Mabul was 'deviant carnal behavior' (*Rashi* on Bereishis, 9:25. *Sanhedrin*, 108a). Nevertheless, the final verdict of the Mabul was due to 'theft' (*Sanhedrin*, ibid: "Even so, the main cause was deviant behavior"). In either case, the Generation of the Flood caused a separation between the Sefiros of Yesod and Malchus, the 'higher waters' and the 'lower waters' respectively. The Zohar says this separation was caused specifically through 'wasting seed' — any act in which one seeks to give without any consideration for a proper 'vessel' to 'receive.' In such a case, it is as if there are no 'feminine' waters present and prepared to receive the outflow of 'masculine' waters. In truth, such 'giving' is actually an expression of self-centered taking, the shadow side of receiving. This is further related to the Torah's prohibition against cross-breeding, in which a particular giver and receiver are not a correcct fit for one another. The result of either scenario is not authentic, deeper connection, but greater disconnection between the upper and lower realms, between soul and body, between masculine and femine energies, between self and other.

The Torah says the Flood occurred due to the fact that, "The whole earth was filled with חמס / Chamas" (*Bereishis*, 6:11). *Chamas* is a form of violent taking, or theft (*Sanhedrin*, 108a). Interestingly, *Cham*, the two-letter root of Chamas, simply means 'heat,' signifying misdirected passion and selfish carnal 'taking.' In fact, according to the Zohar, *Chamas* actually implies "wasted seed," in addition to its literal connotation of thievery. In a Biblical version of a 'return of the repressed,' one of Noach's sons was named Cham, and Rashi, commenting on a mysterious episode in the Torah, says Cham was implicated in a complicated and compromising interaction with his father Noach, drunk in his tent (*Bereishis* 9:25).

Not only did the essential imbalance of that time, which placed a wedge between giving and receiving on all levels from the elemental to the economic to the carnal, prevent greater unity between the upper and lower waters in human-to-human relationships, but also in Divine-human relationships as well. In other words, it disrupted the very possibility for wholesome relationship throughout the heavens and the earth. These various imbalances sweeping across the planet, according to the Medrash, included even harmful interbreeding among animals. This suggests that the fabric of creation itself was impacted by humanity's misalignment (*Beis haLevi*, Noach). Nature itself was affected by this disparity between Yesod and Malchus.

Rashi comments on Bereishis (7:12): And the rain was upon the earth: "Later on the Torah says: 'Now the Flood was [upon the earth].' When He brought them [the rains] down first, He brought them down with *Rachamim* / mercy, so that if they would repent, they would be rains of blessing.

When they did not repent, they became a flood (See *Zohar Chadash*, 28a).

The lower waters that burst forth at the time of the Mabul were hot, as in 'hot-springs' that bubble up from the earth. These scalding lower waters of the Mabul were, on the one hand, an expression of the destructive and consuming heat of unrepentant and misdirected passion that unleashed them as a measure-for-measure consequence of the heat generated by the indulgence of destructive cravings. While on the other hand, without contradicting the above interpretation, the warm waters of the Mabul can also be understood as rehabilitative — a merciful means of Tikkun, bringing together both Gevurah and Chesed. In this sense, the waters were like a vast worldwide Mikvah, a ritual pool of cleansing water which drowned negativity, while also simultaneously restoring purity to the world. Like a Mikvah, the hot waters enabled the masculine and feminine waters to re-unite. And indeed, as the Torah suggests, the lower waters and the upper waters were joined as one.

TWO WATERS & ONE WATERS

Water is the place and element of *Ta'avah* / desire (*Sha'arei Kedusha*, 1:1. *Tanya*, 1). In the beginning of Creation, the Torah says, "The earth was astonishingly empty, and darkness was on the face of the deep, and the spirit of G-d was *Merachefes* / hovering over the face of the water" (1:2). Even before the first openly articulated creation of Light there was already water, representing Divine desire, the arousal of which gave rise to the world.

Water is thus connected to the *Ma'amar Echad* / the First Hidden Essential Utterance of Creation. This 'hidden Ma'amar' is the word *Bereishis* itself.* In fact, at the very moment the Ma'amar *Bereishis* was 'spoken,' water was already revealed; according to the deeper teachings of the Torah, this implies that water, Divine desire, is the meta-root of all Creation.

Various 'reasons'** are offered for why the world came into being, for example, "The nature of Good (G-d) is to give goodness" (*Emek HaMelech*, Sha'ar 1:1. *Derech Hashem. Da'as Tevunos*, 18). According to this view, as Hashem is the Source of Goodness, Hashem fashions a Creation in order to bestow goodness upon it. Another reason given for why such a finite, multi-faceted Creation came into being was "to reveal the complete array and perfection of His powers and deeds." Regarding this, we learn that 'the most dazzling power displayed by the Infinite One was in creating a finite being' (*Eitz Chayim*, Sha'ar 1. Derush Igulim v'Yosher). Alternatively, some posit that Hashem created the world simply "so that we would know Him" (*Zohar* 2, 42b), and acknowledge His existence (*Ramban*, Shemos, 13:16).

The fundamental difficulty with all of these reasons are twofold: a) If the Creator merely created angelic, celestial beings, they

---

* "'*Bereishis* is also a Ma'amar' (*Rosh Hashanah*, 32a), It is the hidden utterance" (*Maharsha*, ad loc.). The Ma'amar Echad is thus the actual word *Bereishis*. Although, according to *Zohar* 3, 11b and *Pirkei d'Rebbe Eliezer*, "Let there be Light" is the Ma'amar Echad.

**Parenthetically, finding anthropomorphic "reasons" already suggests a separation and movement away from the actual status of Unity. Ultimately, there can be no humanly knowable reasons or reasoning behind the creation of an apparent world of duality.

would also be sufficient creation to bestow goodness. In fact, they, even more than human beings, would be consistently more appreciative of the Infinite One's power, certainly they 'know Him' better than we do. And, b) any reason given suggests a 'need' on behalf of the Creator, a need suggests a 'lack,' something that is 'missing' which when added brings about 'completion' — and the Creator, by definition, does not lack.

Regarding this issue, the Alter Rebbe quotes the Medrash (*Tanchumah*, Naso, 16) which states that Creation came into being because "Hashem *desires* to have a *Dirah* / dwelling place *b'Tachtonim* / in the *lower* worlds" (*Tanya*, 36). This is the ultimate purpose behind the creation of this physical, lower world. This is truly a reason beyond all rationale, as the nature of desire is beyond reason (Rebbe Rashab, *Hemshech Samach Vav*, p. 7). Desire, in this sense, is not a rationalizable need, but rather a very personal want.

This supra-rational Divine desire to create is the deepest and innermost root/foundation of all Creation. The first actual 'substance' outside of the void to be mentioned in the account of Creation is water, symbolizing this very desire, present even before creation itself, as it were.

UPPER DESIRES AND LOWER DESIRES: "DO NOT SAY 'WATER! WATER!'"

The meta-root of all desire, and of creation itself, is the One Divine desire. And since, all desire (lower waters) is rooted in the Divine desire (upper waters), there is really only one 'water,' one desire in creation. However, the *Dor haMabul* / Generation of the Flood "separated the Upper and Lower Waters" as the Zohar tells us.

The deepest reason that anyone anywhere ever desires anything, is that, on a deeper level, they desire to fulfil the Divine desire. It is simply a mistaken perception of the natural Oneness of reality that causes them to think that they are actually desiring the food, the new car, or the other person as ends in themselves. These exterior desires are really just 'fallen' attempts to fulfil the One desire, the welcoming and indwelling of the Divine in this world.

This dynamic is compellingly illustrated in a paradigmatic episode recorded in the Gemara, in which, Rabbi Akiva, together with three of his peers, entered into the PaRDeS, the mythic orchard of esoteric secrets regarding consciousness and creation. Aware of the dangers involved in such a rarified ascent of the soul into the meta-physical realms of Torah and reality, Rabbi Akiva warns not to fall into the mistake of dualistic vision, no matter what they may see while in the grips of such a mystical, prophetic-like experience: "When you come to a place of pure marble stones, do not say 'Water! Water!'" (*Chagigah*, 14b). In other words: 'Do not say that there are two waters! Rather, always remember and recognize that there is really no separation between the waters, it is all one water!' (*Zohar* I, 26b. *Tikunei Zohar*, Tikkun 40. *Pardes Rimonim*, Erchei haKinuyim, Mayim).

From the rigidly binary perspective of 'two waters,' the higher waters represent the desire for *Ruchniyus* / spirituality, and the lower waters signify a desire for *Gashmiyus* / materialism. People tend to separate their desires in just this way, and feel that their physical desires are fundamentally in conflict with their higher desires for spiritual truth. In fact, many people don't even think that they have a higher desire at all. This was the exact issue with the *Dor haMabul*, which was completely immersed and absorbed within its own fallen, separative *Ta'avah*.

There are three things that "take a person out of the world," or seem to separate him from perceiving the world as Oneness: *Kinah* / jealousy, *Ta'avah* / desire, and *Kavod* / attachment to honor (*Avos*, 4:21). *Kinah* is the mistake of Kayin and Hevel, Ta'avah, is the mistake of the Dor haMabul, and attachment to Kavod is the mistake of the Generation of the Tower of Babel (*Sefas Emes*, Noach, Tav/Reish/ Nun/Zayin. *Nesivas Shalom*, Noach, 59).

If there had only been the revelation of the *Ma'amar Echad* ('one word' or 'word of oneness') and if Hashem's desire — "the Ruach Elokim that is *Merachefes* on the Mayim" — was alone apparent, there would be no free choice with which to make mistakes, nor would there be any perception of higher and lower desires. There would be only unerring awareness of ultimate Unity. However, as the Mishna teaches, "With ten *Ma'amarim* the world was created. Could it not have been created by just one utterance? Yet (it was created with ten) in order to punish the wicked… and to give reward to the righteous" (*Avos*, 5:1). In other words, free choice — the possibility for righteousness and its opposite, and the interplay between unitive and separative desires — was only possible because the world was created with Ten Utterances.

Therefore, on Day Two of creation, the day of duality and

separation, Hashem says, "Let there be an expanse in the midst of the water, and let there be a separation between water and water… and there appeared a separation between the water that was below the expanse and the water that was above the expanse" (1:6-7). The 'One' water, present even before creation, was separated into two — higher water and lower water, higher desire and lower desire. On the deepest level these waters and desires are always united and remain only One, but, following Day-Two, the appearance of separation is now our default perception, and we must expand and correct it through a path of Tikkun.

After the waters were separated, the lower waters cried out, 'We too wish to be close to the King!' They continued complaining about their unfair treatment until they were assured that they would eventually be offered up on the altar on account of their salt content, and as *Nisuch haMayim* / the water libations of the Sukkos festival (*Tikunei Zohar*, 19b. *Rashi*, Vayikra 2:13. It is interesting to note that this teaching by Chazal is not found in the Talmud or Medrash; yet, it seems to have been known, and thus quoted by Rashi and other Rishonim, such as Rabbeinu Bachya). On one hand, this anecdote represents the lower waters' movement toward their eventual reunification with the higher waters. But, from a deeper perspective, the fact that the lower waters can be brought back up 'in front of the King' means that they are always already one and unified. This furthermore also suggests that we too can also return to the Only One Desire of Hashem, from which we were never really separated.

"דור המבול ברבה קלקלו וברבה נידונו" / the generation of the flood sinned with *Rabah* / excess and were thus punished with *Rabah* / excess" (*Sanhedrin*, 108a). The corruption of the generation of the

Flood is characterized as *Rabah* / excessive, and their punishment is also characterized as *Rabah* / excessive. They corrupted themselves with *Rabah*, with gusto, meaning that the deepest dimensions of their being were activated and implicated in their acts of corruption. They were likewise 'punished' or cleansed with *Rabah*, representing the deepest untapped waters of Hashem's own subconscious desire, as it were. Thus, the waters of the Flood, surging up from the veritable wellsprings of creation, were the necessary Tikkun that cleansed that generation like a worldwide Mikvah; purifying and opening the world to become an intimate dwelling place for the Divine, in the lower realms of physical creation.

CHEIN, GRACE, CHARM, EASE

The name *Noach* is spelled Nun-Ches, which are also the same letters of *Chein*, most often translated as grace, but which means so much more. *Chein* is a kind of charm, charisma, or sense of existential easiness. Interestingly, Ches-Nun also stands for *Chatas Ne'urim* / the 'sins of one's youth' — usually defined as the wasting of vital seed, signifying a misalignment and disconnection between the giver and the receiver, as discussed previously. We learn from this that Chein is gained or increased when a person works on perfecting and balancing their attribute of Yesod, meaning their intimate energies and abilities to connect and sustain meaningful, reciprocal relationships with self and others. A person who lives effortlessly, expressing a unitive flow from feeling to word to action, manifesting and modeling an authentic connection between giver

and receiver, free from disruptive desires, torturous inner dichot-
omies, or unhealthy misalignments, is someone who has achieved
and surely exudes great Chein.

A careful reading of the portion of Noach reveals a pervasive
pattern of contrasts between words containing the letters מח /
Mem-Ches and נח / Nun-Ches.

The root letters Ches-Mem appear repeatedly as *Cham* / heat,
as well as being the name of Noach's ill-fated son. Additionally,
the flood is justified in the Torah on account of the overwhelming *Chamas* / violent selfishness and thievery of that generation.
Furthermore, Mem-Ches also appears in the word *Emchah*, when
Hashem says "I will אמחה / *Emchah* / erase (that generation)" (*Bere-*
ishis, 6:7) on account of its *Chamas*. Ches-Mem, then, alludes to
Cham, understood as a negative, selfish 'heat' that 'forcefully' over-
takes one and leaves them feeling empty and 'erased' after its ex-
penditure — as there is no real relationship between the giver and
receiver, and thus no chance of further, future life or vitality. In this
state, one's 'giving' devolves into 'taking,' cutting off all flow and
connection, leaving one isolated and more alone than they were
before they acted on such desire.

The opposite of *Cham* / negative heat is Nun-Ches — spelling
Noach or *Nach* / comfort, and *Chein* / grace. Noach sent the raven
out of the ark from the חלון / *Chalon* / window "that he had made."
The word *Chalon* is composed of the words חן לו / *Chein Lo* / he
has Chein. This refers to Noach, who 'made a window' in his ark,
through which he could see and be seen by the world outside of
himself. When one locks themselves away in a closed system —

insulated from, unaware of, and opaque to the needs and desires of others — their energies and actions remain static and stuck in a loop of self-referentiality. This generates the selfish passions of *Ches-Mem*. By carving out and creating a window in the ark, Noach literally and figuratively let the light in, as well as provided himself with a medium, through which he too could project his inner light out into the world. This constructive concern for the world and others beyond one's own small circle generates the comforting charisma of *Nun-Ches*.

The passionate heat referred to as *Cham* is a one-dimensional emotion — completely focused on fulfilling the desires of the Mashpia, the giver, with no consideration for the Mekabel, the receiver. It is totally selfish, and thus entirely 'erases' the receiver. Chein and Nach, both states of true wellbeing, are the result of an achieved balance between authentic giving and appropriate withholding, with mindful consideration for the desires and experiences of the Mekabel. Giving from this place is truly *comforting* and *graceful*.

One of the names for Moshiach is מנחם / *Menachem*, spelled Mem-Nun-Ches-Mem (*Sanhedrin*, 98b). This combination of letters implies that Moshiach is able to elevate the paradigm of Ches-Mem (Tohu) into Ches-Nun (Tikkun). We too, in the deepest levels of our souls, have the ability to channel and elevate the *Cham*, the heat of this world, to a place of *Nach* and *Chein*, which is נייחא לעליונים נייחא לתחתונים / *NeiCha l'Elyonim v'Neicha l'Tachtonim* / pleasant Above and pleasant below (*Medrash Rabbah*, Bereishis, 30:5). This is the supreme pleasure of the ultimate bridging and unification of higher and lower waters.

The true attractiveness of a person, beneath the skin of surface beauty, is their Chein, also translated as charm. Sometimes people look good on the outside, yet there is something disconcerting or off-putting about them. And sometimes a person does not have the external appearance appreciated by their dominant culture, and yet people gravitate towards them nonetheless. Chein is something that is not quantifiable or measurable. It is a projection of something from within a person, independent of external appearances.

Real charm comes from being careful not to selfishly disperse creative power through acts such as חטאת נעורים / Chatas Ne'urim. The Gemara says, "A person who has Chein is a *Yerei Shamayim* / a person in awe of Heaven" (*Sukkah*, 49b). A Yerei Shamayim is a person who acts with inner integrity and alignment, someone who is attuned to their deeper purpose for being and creatively expresses their life's purpose in the very way they conduct their life.

The concept of Chein is also associated with Yoseph (*Bereishis*, 39:4). Yoseph is the ancestral embodiment of Yesod. Like Noach, he is one of the very few characters in Tanach who is referred to explicitly as a Tzadik. Incidentally, Menasheh, the first-born son of Yoseph, is the representative tribe of the month of Cheshvan, as we will explore.

There are seven archetypal Biblical personalities, and each of them embodies one of the seven emotion-based Sefiros. Avraham is *Chesed* / kindness and giving, Yitzchak is *Gevurah* / strength and severity, and so on. Yoseph, as mentioned, is the embodiment of the Sefira of *Yesod* / focus and intimacy. In the Torah's narrative, Yoseph's Chein and powers of 'connectivity' come from his ability to avoid illicit intimacy with Potiphar's wife. When Potiphar's wife physically grabs him and tries to seduce him, he musters his inner strength and focus, and flees from her grasp. This episode leads to his imprisonment, where, because of his Chein (*Bereishis*, 39:21), other inmates are drawn to him as a wise interpreter of dreams. Interpreting the dreams of the ministers of the king leads to him eventually decoding the dream of the king himself, and thereby rising to prominence as the king's vizier.

The great sage Rav Yochanan, whose name contains the word Chein, says regarding himself, "I am from the seed of Yoseph" (*Berachos*, 20a). Yochanan is connected with Chein (*Berachos*, 57a). The truth is anyone, even someone whose name does not contain the letters of *Ches-Nun*, can cultivate and maintain some measure of Chein.

On a psycho-structural level, Chein is the quality of alignment, where there is no dichotomy between what a person knows, feels, and does. Children have a lot of Chein, because they act honestly according to how they feel, and what they know. Yoseph radiated Chein. His aura sparkled with an almost childlike quality (See *Bereishis*, 37:2). He knew inwardly that he was destined for greatness, and he was not shy about it. With a childlike naivete, he paraded and expressed his deepest desires and dreams. His brothers were jealous, and thought he was arrogant, but his father knew his prophetic dreams were true, and that one day their authenticity would be revealed to all (*Rashi*, Bereishis, 37:11).

Regarding Noach the Torah explicitly says, "Noach found Chein in the eyes of Hashem" (*Bereishis*, 5:8). This was his very nature, encoded directly into his name. Noach was born Tamim. And he maintained a focus on righteousness, in contrast to his generation of completely disconnected, self-serving intimacy and theft. Thus he was able to unify both upper and lower waters. However, he did, in the end, fail to inspire his generation, and this is why the Zohar calls him a רעיא שטיא / *Raya Shatya* / foolish shepherd. As righteous and filled with Chein as Noach was, he was not on the level to save humanity, beyond his own family, from its own misaligned passions and perversions.

After the Flood — meaning after the world was healed of the rift between upper and lower waters, after the archetypal giver and receiver have been brought back into a reciprocal relationship with each other Noach emerges from the ark and brings an offering that is a *Re'ach* הניחח / *haNicho'ach La'Hashem* / a pleasant aroma for Hashem (*Bereishis*, 8:21). Within the word *Nicho'ach* are the words *Noach* and *Chein*. Noach's Chein reaches Heaven and exudes an altogether pleasant aroma.

Nicho'ach is generally translated as 'pleasant aroma' — which is connected to Cheshvan, as will be explored shortly — but *Nicho'ach* also suggests a sense of ease. In our own lives, when we have done a Tikkun for our own misaligned expressions of creativity and passion, we also experience a *No'ach* — a 'gentle caress' of inner-peace, a subtle sense of ease and release. When we live with Chein in a state of free-flowing integrity, with less existential conflict and anxiety, we too feel lighter and easier, and can thus navigate the currents of our life with increased faith and effortless joy.

THE TWO LETTER 'NUN'S

Chein is comprised of a Ches — as in Cheshvan, being the eighth month of the year — and a Nun, which is the letter of the month. As mentioned, there are two types of Nun: the common Nun (נ) and the Final Nun (ן). The common Nun appears to have fallen and its leg is collapsed, while the Final Nun stands up straight, rooted deep within. The fallen or buckling Nun is the 'struggler,' the person who deals with darkness, strife and complication, and then overcomes. The straight Nun is the person who lives with more ease and Chein, the *Tamim* / perfect or straightforward one. In his wholesome simplicity, this person can be slightly naïve, like Yoseph. Both Yoseph and Noach were born with supernatural gifts, as Noach is born *Mahul* / circumcised, and Yoseph is naturally very beautiful, they both ooze with Chein. These physical traits represent a deeper spiritual reality, that of their souls.

A twisted or buckled Nun is a person who lives in the face of falling, but also continually struggles, gets up, and starts again. This is a person who never gives up and recognizes that even "A *Tzadik* / righteous person falls seven (many) times and gets back up" (*Mishlei* 24:16). In this context, what defines someone as a Tzadik is not regarding *whether* he falls, rather, it is that even when he is falling he does not give up, he summons his inner resources, roots himself firmly in his convictions, and stands up straight again, ready to move forward with higher purpose and deep humility. A deeper reading of this Pasuk is that it is not just the resilience to get back up that makes someone a Tzadik, it is actually the 'seven' falls themselves that make one a Tzadik. From this perspective, greatness actually comes from falling and entering the dark space found in the night of the soul, feeling deeply its existential estrangement and lack. This is what builds character, and brings out the light that shines from darkness, a light brighter than any other in all the worlds. This is the nature of the struggler. And it is this strength and perseverance that we must develop in Cheshvan — the quiet, dark month of potential falling and descent, the month of tapping in, going deep, getting up, and standing tall again.

Yet, there is also the possibility of the straight Nun — or the twisted Nun that has been straightened out. This is also called the נחש ברח / *Nachash Bariach* / straight — gliding snake and the נחש עקלתון / *Nachash Aklason* / twisted, coiled snake (*Yeshayahu*, 27:1). A 'straight Nun' person is like Yoseph, one who seems to float through life, almost like an uninterrupted dream. Hardships and struggles seem to just bounce off them, and they maintain balance.

Yoseph is numerically 156 (Yud/10, Vav/6, Samach/60 and Pei/80 = 156), which is equal to the word *Tziyon* / Zion. *Tziyon* is spelled with four letters: Tzadi (also called Tzadik), Yud (which is a point or very small line), Vav (a longer line), and a final Nun (which is an even longer line extending all the way down below the baseline). These letter forms illustrate the type of Tzadik that Yoseph was. He was rooted in the Yud, the Above, his higher mission and purpose. His life was one continuous line from the Yud to a Vav, and even further until the final Nun. He went from the Holy Land, as the favored son of the world's greatest spiritual master, all the way to being indefinitely incarcerated in a dark dungeon in the lowest foreign land, surrounded by criminals; and there he brought G-d's light along with him no matter what situation he was in. The point of his life just kept on extending lower and lower, but without any internal twists, turns, or falls. He never had to struggle or get up, he was always where he was supposed to be. Although his life was filled with external drama, he consistently maintained an inner alignment and a perfected attribute of Yesod. "A Tzadik that is Yesod" is one that exudes Chein and lives in what appears to be an effortlessness flow, with little or no internal battles or existential ups and downs. Such a Tzadik is always steady, straight, standing tall.

DEEPER INTO THE TWO TYPES OF NUN

Nun is one of the only letters in the Aleph Beis whose 'filling' — the spelling of the letter itself — consists of the same letter. Whereas, for example, the filling of Aleph is 'Aleph-Lamed-Pei', the filling of Nun is simply 'Nun-Nun'. This doubling alludes to the two kinds of Nun: the regular, bent Nun symbolizing *Nefilah* / falling, and the final Nun symbolizing digging deep and standing tall. The fallen or bent Nun also corresponds to the *Nachash* / snake of the Tree of Knowledge of separation. The Final Nun corresponds to Moshiach, the fully rectified state of this Nachash, the state of Inner Integrity and Divine Unity.

What is the Nachash? The Torah describes him as *Arum* (*Bereishis*, 3:1). Literally, the word *Arum* means sly, in the sense of manipulative and sneaky (*Berachos*, 17a, Rashi). But what does the Nachash symbolize for us? The Seforno writes that the Nachash represents false imagination. The snake had an over-active imagination and was trapped in a world of fantasy. The snake — i.e., over-active imagination — comes to Chavah and inculcates her with grandiose imagery, telling her that Hashem told her not to eat from the tree because "Hashem knows that when you eat from it, your eyes will be opened, and you will be like G-d" (*Bereishis*, 3:5). The snake attempts to inject Chavah with a poisonously presumptuous vision of herself by telling her that the reason she was told not to eat from the Tree of Knowledge was that if she did, she would become all-powerful.

Our own overactive imagination and fantasy, our inner snake, clouds and distorts our accurate vision of reality. This ego-based faculty ends up feeding us only what our ego wants, or, in a distorted way, what our ego is afraid of. In our fantasies we are either all-powerful and important or utterly worthless and destitute. If your ego is focusing on money, for example, it may create imagery of you becoming a billionaire, or of you losing your job and living on the street. This is the danger of the 'snake;' it pulls a person out from a clear perception of reality and inflates his ego with exaggerated grandiosity or crippling fear.

Fantasy is born when we feel that we have total control of how our life is going to unfold. If we have a 'healthy' sense of fantasy, we may imagine the best, or even most fantastical future for ourselves. If our sense of fantasy is unhealthy, we may find ourselves fantasizing about the most horrific possible futures. Either way, such imaginary worlds are ego-based and self-infatuated. How do we tame, overcome or rectify our inner Nachash? How do we break our illusions of control over our experience and the world?

BOWING TO BREAK 'SNAKE CONSCIOUSNESS'

During the Amidah prayer when we recite *Modim* / we humbly submit to You… we bow our heads. About this motion, our sages teach, "He who does not bow at Modim, after seven years of interment, his lifeless spine will transform into a snake" (*Baba Kama,* 15b). One meaning of this is that the act of bowing ensures that a man's spine will not completely dissolve in the grave and he will be able to experience resurrection. But what does this mean?

In Bereishis the snake gives voice to a desire for self-sufficiency. *'You can become like G-d, take complete control of your life, just eat this fruit.'* These ego-stroking visions of grandeur were the metaphorical snake-oil being sold in the Garden (of Eden).

To combat this idolatry of the ego we humbly bow during the Amidah. When we reach the prayer of *Modim* / acknowledgement or submission, we bend our spines to facilitate a state of *Bitul* / self-nullification and humble submission in the presence of the All-Mighty. By bowing, we thereby surrender our sense of full control and acknowledge that there is a higher guiding Hand in our lives and in the world. Although some things are certainly in our control, and we do have free-choice, in a state of humility we can more clearly make the distinction between what is and what is not in our control. The physical movement of bowing can thus help break the subtle, subconscious fantasy that we are all-knowing or all-powerful.

This is not to say that we have no control over ourselves or over our lives; we are at least potentially in control of our attitudes and responses to events. But what is thrown at us — by other people (e.g. insults or praises) or by 'the world' (e.g. the weather and the stock market) or even by our own unrelenting thoughts — is ultimately beyond our control. And so, with this distinction in mind, we humbly submit and surrender to the Master of the Universe and say, 'Modim — thank You. We are grateful for what we have, and humbled to live in Your Presence!' On the deepest level of Modim, we recognize that everything which happens is, was, and will be from Hashem alone. This awareness is the spiritual antidote for the bite of the proverbial snake.

THE SECRET OF BOWING, BREAKING, AND ELEVATING SNAKE ENERGY

Death, and the consciousness of death, was first introduced by Adam and Chavah's eating from the Tree of Knowledge and duality. This reality-shifting event occurred ultimately because Adam and Chava succumbed to their egoic fantasies of 'snake consciousness.' Interestingly, according to the Zohar, whoever does not bow in the Modim prayer will not rise up from the dead at the time of the Great Resurrection (*Zohar* 2, p.100). But what does all this talk of death and resurrection have to do with the spine?

According to the Medrash, the resurrection and reemergence of the body (*Bereishis*, 28:3. *Vayikra*, 18:1) will sprout forth from the immortal *Etzem Luz* / the Luz bone. This is a small 'bone' or particle in a person's back that is believed to be located either on the top, or bottom, of the spinal column (*HaAruch*, Erech Luz. *Likutei Torah*, Arizal, Na'ch, Shoftim. *Avodas haKodesh*, 2:40). The Luz bone is rooted in the paradigm of the Tree of Life (*Eliyah Rabah*, Orach Chayim 300: 3), signifying the Divine Unity within us. It is beyond the effects of duality and separation stemming from the Tree of Knowledge of

Good and evil — including the disintegration of the body called death. In other words: There is a part of us that is beyond the ego, beyond snake consciousness, beyond our distorted fantasies, and essentially beyond physicality itself. It is that part of us which is always whole, perfect and unified.

It is through the Luz bone that the soul receives great spiritual pleasure in the next world, and yet it can also be the medium of great suffering, i.e., learning the hard way. This suffering or 'refusal to learn' is related to 'not bowing in the Modim prayer;' not humbling oneself in gratitude and self-nullification before the Infinite One. In the words of the *Avodas haKodesh*, not bowing in Modim "makes the essence of one's existence fall into the reality of the Nachash, which causes death and the cessation of all sensation" (*Avodas Hakodesh*, 2:40). Without sensation we have no way of knowing that we have fallen, and therefore no urge or determination to arise; we are then, therefore, as good as dead. The acknowledgment and gratitude expressed by bowing in Modim during prayer is a sign of life and vitality.

Regarding the primordial snake in the Garden of Eden, when Chavah was confronted by Hashem for what she had done she immediately exclaimed, "הנחש השיאני / *haNachash Hishiani* / the Snake has deceived me" (*Bereishis*, 3:13). The word השיאני / *Hishiani* is a *Notarikon* / composite of the words יש אני / *Yesh Ani* / I am a Yesh, an egoic 'something.' This is the essential deception of snake-consciousness: the ultimate sovereignty of an isolated ego. In this fantasy, one appears to exist apart from all others and from the Ultimate 'I' of Hashem. Such self-centered separation, or 'something-thingness,' is an illusion.

The Nachash is, in a sense, an outside voice, an 'external' reality to the inner truth of Adam and Chavah, it therefore represents Yesh. But the core of Adam and Chavah is in fact *Ayin* / humble no-thingness, the transparency of ego. The numerical value of Adam is 45, which is the same as the value of the word *Mah* / What. *Mah*, a question, refers to the state of Ayin, the openness of not-knowing. This is true human consciousness, free from deception; as nothing, we are transparent to, and unified with, the Ultimate 'I' of Hashem, and this is the backbone of our, as well as all, existence.

One of the Snake's primary powers is Turning *Tov* / good into *Ra* / bad. The Ramdu (*Moshia Chosim*, Shemuel 1:25) writes that the idea of *K'fui Tovah* / ingratitude, is linked to the Snake. According to the Medrash, the Snake, similar to humanity, was originally created with an erect posture and with the power of speech (*Sotah*, 9b. *Medrash Rabbah*, Bereishis, 20:5. See, *Likutei Sichos*, 10 p. 13). Instead of being grateful for these gifts, and using them for the good, the Snake nurtured the jealousies and fantasies of Adam and Chavah, seducing them to sin. This is understood by the sages as a supreme act of K'fui Tovah, which is, "*Meishiv Ra Tachas Tovah* / repaying good with evil" (*Mishlei*, 17:13).

Thus, bowing and actively expressing *Hakaras haTov* / acknowledgment of the good breaks the spiritual spell of the Snake. *Modim* means to humbly submit, and humility leads one to be *Makir Tov* / appreciative of good. Acknowledging and retrieving the kernel of the good from the shell of apparent bad is an antidote to eating from the Tree of Conflating Good with evil.

When Adam (who was originally both male and female) first gained human consciousness, they observed Creation and declared to all living creatures, "Come let us bow… before Hashem" (*Zohar* 3, p.107b). This is in sharp contrast to the first utterance of the Nachash, who turned to Chavah and said, 'Go ahead, eat from this Tree — it will make you like G-d!' (*Bereishis*, 3:5). Whereas true human consciousness, the soul, speaks from a state of ultimate humility, the external voice of the ego, the Nachash, always seeks self-aggrandizement and substantiation of its own sovereignty.

The Tree of Knowledge of Good and evil is the source of ego, separation, and eventual death. Whereas the Tree of Life is the paradigm of unity which is accessed through *Bitul* / humility and acknowledgment of the Higher reality of eternity. As we have been discussing, we bow when we recite the prayer *Modim Anachnu Lach* / We submit to You, and to You alone…" By bending our spine and affirming our submission to the Infinite One, we 'break' and humble our inner snake, our deceptive egoic separateness. By lowering ourselves in this way, we paradoxically reveal our underlying immortality and unity with Hashem. This is how we claim our birthright, which is a conscious, innate connection with Gan Eden and the Tree of Life.

According to the sages the spine carries sperm, a snake-like energy, from the brain to the lower parts of the body (*Tosefos*, Nidah, 14a). It is thus the channel for both G-d-like creative potential, as well as the seeds of self-centered delusion. A Tzadik is one who has rectified the attribute of Yesod so that the flow of procreative energy is in dynamic alignment with the rest of the Sefiros (*Regel Yeshara*, (Dinov) Tzadik 4). Interestingly, the letter Tzadi(k) is shaped, says the Zohar, like a Yud — which represents the *Tipah* / drop of seed — on top of a Nun (*Zohar* 1, 2b. In fact, two Yud's -and one backwards. Hakdamah, *Zohar. Pardas Rimonim*, Sha'ar HaOsyos, 21. *Chasam Sofar,* Yorah De'ah, 266). This letter-form is thus a diagram of the seed of the Yud (giver) flowing directly into the *Nukvah* / female (receiver), in a harmonious manner (*Magen Avos* (Trisk) *Tikkun haGadol shel Shalosh Eser Midos*). This is an essential aspect of a Tzadik, the holistic integration of all his energies, including the procreative, within a selfless and spiritual life. This integration allows a Tzadik to live in a constant state of *Modim* / humility, gratefulness, and thus unity. When our inner core of unity is revealed outwardly, we embody and express our soul, or inner Tree of Life, in our day to day life. Our whole body is thus transformed into the immortal Luz bone; in fact, we become the Luz bone (*Medrash Talpiyos*, Os Yud. *Maor vaShemesh*, Parshas Vayechi). This is why it is taught that a Tzadik's body is preserved even long after it has been interred (*Medrash Tehilim*, 119:9). In this state of unity, even the physical form does not need to dissolve back into separate elements.

However, if we heed the Snake's arrogant suggestions even subtly, snake-energy rises up the spine from the lower regions of the body, giving us a false fantasy of being all-powerful. Then we become like Pharoah, Chas veShalom, the embodiment of the Nachash, who made the grandiose claim of being a deity. Such egoic power cannot be sustained, and will eventually experience a *Nefilah* / falling down, and ultimately death. However, if we consciously bow in Modim during prayer, releasing all egoic power as we lower our head and stretch our spine, energy moves instead from the brain down to the lower parts of the body, elevating and integrating our vital energies and desires, channeling our whole being to connect with and serve the Infinite One.

After we bow down in Modim, we say Hashem's name while returning back to an upright posture. Regarding this motion, fascinatingly, our sages teach us that we should rise with a 'snake-like movement' (*Berachos*, 12b). So, then, we bow to 'break' the energy of the snake, that of self-centered fantasy, and then we rise up and out of the bowed posture, like a snake raising itself erect. This upward movement symbolizes the raising of the fallen Nachash energy into a redeemed and reintegrated state of illumination. The letter Nun is also connected to the spine (*Sefer haBahir*, 84). Once our spine, containing our inner Nachash as it were, has bowed down into the shape of the Fallen Nun, we then lift ourselves up and elevate the Nachash, the transformed energy, standing straight while firmly grounded like the final Nun. The two Nuns thus become an illustration of the process of humble submission trans-forming into upright integrity.

Modim, in numerical value, is 100 (Mem/40 + Vav/6 + Daled/4 + Yud/10 + Mem/40 = 100). This corresponds to the two Nuns, as each Nun equals 50. In the act of bowing during Modim there is first the humbling of the 'falling Nun,' followed by tapping in and the standing up of the 'straight Nun.'

The Nun at the beginning of the word *Nachash* is the fallen Nun, whereas the Nun at the end of the word Cheshvan is the redeemed Final Nun. Through humbling and channeling the vital energy of our inner Nachash, we can transform the fallen Nun to the upright Nun, and thus convert the unredeemed, bitterness of Mar Cheshvan into the sweet elevation of Ram Cheshvan.* Humility is the secret of "going low to get high." And getting up after falling down is the Avodah of this month.

THE INNER MOSHIACH

The upright Final Nun signifies the Era of Moshiach. According to one opinion the name of Moshiach will be *Yinon* (*Sanhedrin,* 98b), as hinted in Tehilim: יהי שמו לעולם לפני־שמש ינון שמו / *Y'hi Shemo leOlam, Lifnei Shemesh Yinon Shemo* / May his name endure forever; may his name be continued as long as the sun (*Tehilim,* 72:17). It may also be that Moshiach Ben Yoseph is Yinon, as he 'comes before the sun;' in this case, "the sun" would be an allusion to Moshiach ben David (*Medresh Rabbah,* Bereishis, 31:10. *Megaleh Amukos,* Vayechi). The word *Yinon* / continued can also mean 'from Nun.' From this perspective, Moshiach will come from the redeemed paradigm of the Final Nun.

We all have a spark of Moshiach within us. Our inner redeemer or *Moshiach haP'ratis* is the spark within our soul that is beyond fallings or exiles. It is always already redeemed, and it is the deepest level of who we are (*Maor Einayim,* Pinchas. The Rebbe, *Kuntres Inyana Shel Toras haChassidus*). One of the secrets of releasing this inner power is to always get up as soon as we have fallen, or to even catch ourselves as we begin to fall.

The coming of Moshiach, who represents the *Gemar haTikkun* / complete rectification of life, is only relevant after the fall that occurred within the Garden of Eden. To explain: before Adam

---

* Mar, in the language of the Gemara, actually means 'exchanged' *Rashi,* Chulin, 94a. *Tosefos,* Bechoros, 30a. *Toesfos,* Sanhedrin, 64a.

and Chavah ate from the Tree of Knowledge, their bodies were expanded from the earth to the Heavens (*Sanhedrin*, 38b. *Chagigah*, 12a. *Pirkei d'Rebbe Eliezer*, Chap. 11), from one end of the world to the next. After they ate from the Tree of Knowledge, their bodies as well as their consciousness shrank radically. This constituted a 'fall' of the human stature. All souls, which were attached to Adam's body, fell into Kelipah, and required cleansing and Tikkun. It follows that the *Gemar haTikkun* / complete rectification is defined as 'getting back up after the fall,' or reclaiming our original stature, reaching from Heaven to earth. Moshiach will usher in a state where we, and the whole world, will be standing upright, in a fully expanded stature and posture, just like in Gan Eden.

Our greatness is revealed by our ability to bounce back, to never give up, and to always try again. If you have fallen, and even fallen hard, pick yourself up and begin again. You will subliminally inspire others to do the same, and you will bring more light of redemption into the world. This is the process of transforming the 'fallen' Nun to the Final Nun.

Eventually, through the 'getting up' of enough people, a critical mass will engender the revelation of the *Moshiach Kelalis* / universal Redeemer. Then the Third Holy Temple will be built and dedicated in the month of Cheshvan, the month of getting up after falling. This is the rebuilding of the "fallen Sukkah of David" by the Moshiach, who is also referred to as the "fallen one." Without the proverbial fall, there is no need for the redemptive work of Moshiach. From this we learn that it is the fall itself which provides us with the opportunity to rise above our prior perspectives and positions.

This power to get up arises from a deep place within us, one which we may not have even known we possessed before tapping into it out of necessity. In this profound resurgence of will to make an extra push, our true greatness is revealed. It may feel like we need to muster a supernatural power to get up, and get up, and get up again. The first time one falls, one may feel inspired and energized to get up and try again. But if one has fallen "seven times" at some point one may want to say, 'Enough! I don't have the strength and stamina to try again. How can I live like this the rest of my life? I am simply not Tzadik material.' This is the 'external' voice of the Nachash trying to inject a poisonous fantasy of futility.

On the other hand, when a person does succeed in picking himself up off the floor and reclaiming his full human stature, he may feel as if he has superpowers and supreme control over his or her life. This is the Nachash again, attempting to intoxicate you with visions of grandeur. The skeleton key to both of these traps is the humility of Modim, in which we open our mind and body to recognize the Transcendent power that uplifts us. Before we get up, we should say, with confidence, 'I can do this!' After we get up, we should say, with humility and gratitude, 'Hashem, You alone are the source of this power!'

Cheshvan is the 8th month of the year. Numerically the letter Nun is 50. Both 50 and 8 are beyond the natural cycle of seven (8 = 7 +1, 50 = 7 x 7 + 1), and thus, they both symbolize a transcendence of self and the natural world. There will be eight strings on the harp of Moshiach (*Eiruchin*, 13b). In this month of Cheshvan we must actively work within the natural world, self-generating, inspiring and uplifting ourselves and others. But the main *Koach* / power of the month is rooting ourselves in a transcendent, supernatural will and energy to arise after we have stumbled.

When the Divine name *Adon-oi* is spelled out in full (spelling out the names of the letters Aleph-Dalet-Nun-Yud), there are twelve letters. These twelve letters correspond to the twelve months of the year: 1-Aleph, 2-Lamed, 3-Pei, 4-Dalet, 5-Lamed, 6-Tav, 7-Nun, 8-Vav, 9-Nun, 10-Yud, 11-Vav, and 12-Dalet. In this order, Cheshvan corresponds to the letter Vav, a letter that stands upright, much like the final Nun. However, the Final Nun reaches lower than the Vav, implying that it is the Final Nun which brings the Divine light from Above all the way down into this world. The previous letter in the sequence is a regular or 'collapsed' Nun, alluding once again to our inherent ability, shining in this month, to rise up after falling or bowing, and to bring down the light of the Creator into creation.

NAME OF THE MONTH

CCORDING TO THE TORAH, NAMES ARE VERY powerful (*Yumah*, 83b. *Tanchuma*, Hazinu. *Berachos*, 7b). Comprised as they are of Hebrew letters, they represent and define the energy or attributes of that which is named (*Tanya*, Sha'ar HaYichud Veha'emunah, 1). Our names, for instance, unlock and reveal hidden potentials present within our own spiritual makeup. Similarly, names of other people, places, and periods of time provide subtle hints as to their deeper purpose or poetic significance. Additionally, changing one's name is akin to a kind of rebirth; some might even say that a change of name initiates a change of *Mazal* (*Rashi*, Bereishis 15:5. *Rosh Hashanah*, 16b. *Yerushalmi*, Shabbos, 6:39. *Ramah*, Yoreh Deah, 335:10).

Each month of the year has a distinct name, and every name has a meaning. The current names we have for the months were imported into our tradition, upon our return to Israel from the Babylonian Exile. They can in fact be traced to ancient Babylonian or Akkadian names (*Yerushalmi*, Rosh Hashanah, 1:2, *Medrash Rabbah*, Bereishis, 48:9). In the times before the Babylonian Exile, the names of the months were mostly known by their number in the sequence of the year. For example, the month of Av was called the Fifth Month, and Cheshvan was known as the Eighth Month.

Even though prior to the Babylonian Exile Cheshvan was called the Eighth Month, in Tanach it was also called ירח בול / *Yerech Bul* / the moon of *Bul* (*Melachim* 1, 6:38. Rashi, ad loc). The word *Bul* comes from the word *Balah* / withers, since Cheshvan is a time when the grasses have withered and expired in the fields.

'Bul' is also related to the word *Mabul*, flood, as the Medrash points out. Indeed, the Mabul, the Great Flood, began on the 17th of Cheshvan and finally ended a year later on the 27th of Cheshvan. The Mem (which equals 40) in *Mabul* represents the 40 days of rain which fell during the Flood (*Yalkut Shimoni*, Melachim, 184). Another Medrash tells us (*Tanchuma*, Noach, 11), up until the year that Shlomo haMelech built the Beis haMikdash, the rains of the Mabul returned every year for 40 days. Only when he built the Beis haMikdash did those rains stop. Thus he called the month *Bul* (without the Mem — i.e. without the forty days of rain), as it says (*Melachim* 1, 6:38), "And in the eleventh year, in the month of בול / Bul, which is the eighth month, the House (Beis haMikdash) was finished throughout all the parts thereof."

The first letter of the Torah is Beis, the last letter of the Torah is Lamed, and the middle letter is Vav (The Vav in the word *Gachon*. *Kidushin*, 30b). Together, these letters spell the word *Bul*. "For when the Torah was given to Israel the sound thereof traveled from one end of the earth to the other, and all the heathen kings were seized with trembling in their palaces…. They all assembled around the wicked Bilam and asked him, 'What is this tumultuous noise that we have heard? Perhaps a *MaBul* / flood is coming upon the world!'" (*Zevachim*, 116a).

Why do the nations of the world think that another MaBul is coming when the Torah is being given? And why is *(Ma)Bul* encoded in the first, middle, and last letters of the Torah? Because the Torah is a positive MaBul; its light floods the *Tzura* / form of the world and transforms it into a shining, holy, fitting Tzura. The Torah reveals the path of *Teshuvah* / returning to who we really are after having fallen; thus revealing an order beyond the natural order of strict cause and effect. One tool that the Torah suggests for Teshuvah is to immerse ourselves in the waters of a Mikvah in order to regenerate ourselves.

After the destruction of the Beis haMikdash that Shlomo haMelech built, and within the years of the Babylonian Exile, the eighth month began to be called by an Aramaic name, *Cheshvan*, or *Mar Cheshvan* / Bitter Cheshvan. There are sources suggesting that this may have originally been one word, *Marcheshvan*, and only later did it become two separate words. Today most people, by Divine providence, call it simply *Cheshvan*, dropping *Mar* all together.

The word *Mar* can also mean drop, as in a drop of water (*Yeshayahu*, 40:15). Appropriately then, *Mar Cheshvan* can also mean

Rainy Cheshvan, alluding to its status as the official beginning of the rainy season in the Land of Israel (*Pri Chadash* on Even Ezra, 126:7).

Another word which is very similar to Marcheshvan is *Marches-hes* / stirring in the heart, or an internal whispering. This word is also connected to *Chash* / quiet (*Menachos*, 63a). Also, from the perspective of Hebrew, *Cheshvan* contains the word *Chash*. Indeed it is a month that is 'silent' or devoid of holidays. This lack of spiritually stimulating days is part of its dangerous potential for 'falling,' but it is also part of its empowering opportunity for actual-izing our ability to self-generate and 'get up' following any such fall. The letters of the word *Cheshvan* (Ches, Shin, Nun) also contain the word *Nachash* / snake, alluding to the snake energy embedded in this month, as discussed previously, that's quietly waiting for us to elevate and transform it for the good.

Numerically, the word *Cheshvan* is 364 (Ches/8 + Shin/300 + Vav/6 + Nun/50 = 364) This number is one of only a few numerical values quoted in the Gemara. Yuma, 20a, tells us that *HaSatan* / the satan equals 364. This reveals the spiritual challenge of Cheshvan — the potential 'fall' caused by the *Yetzer haRa* / negative inclination, also referred to as *Satan* (*Baba Basra*, 16a). The negative snake energy in Cheshvan is potentially 'satanic' if we chronically refuse to learn from it and elevate it.

The three main letters of the word *Cheshvan* (all but the Vav) spell *Choshen* / breastplate. *Choshen* also shares the same letters with the word *Nachash*. Both of these words have a *Gematriya* / numerical value of 358. The word *Moshiach* / Messiah also equals 358 (*Sefer haLikutim*, Shoftim, 5), again illuminating the code within Cheshvan for redeeming snake energy and moving ourselves from the collapsed Nun to the Final, elevated, rooted Nun. Let us now look closer at how the Choshen factors into this code.

The Choshen was the mystical breastplate of the *Cohen Gadol /* High Priest. Upon the breastplate there were gems inscribed with the names of the Tribes of Israel. The breastplate was used for 'visual' divination, as it were. The priest would pose questions of national consequence, such as whether to go to war or not, and the letters on the Choshen would light up to reveal an oracular answer to such questions, thus acting as a national source of prophetic instruction. The priest would therefore receive prophetic insight through his higher intuition and redeemed (Nachash) imagination by meditating on the lights and letters of the Choshen, which represents the clarification and elevation of the negative imagination of the Nachash.

Manipulating people by appealing to their unrectified sense of imagination is what the Nachash is all about. The vast power of imagination can of course be positive or negative. When we are the riders of the 'snake' of imagination, controlling and guiding it, it can bring great benefit (*Moreh Nevuchim*, 2:30). However, when our unhinged imagination is 'riding' and guiding us, as in the narrative in the Garden of Eden, it signals the beginning of a spiritual downfall. The Nachash is thus the source of human degradation, while at the same time, paradoxically, it also has the same numerical value as Moshiach, the redemption and elevation of humanity through the refinement and rectification of the imagination.

Today, although we lack a physical Choshen, we still have powerful ways to tap into our rectified imagination, such as imaginative Torah study, visionary prayer, and creative contemplation. Additionally, the coiling of the Tefilin around our arm and head represents the harnessing of the Nachash for *Kedushah* / snake for Holiness. The Mitzvah and practice of wrapping Tefilin is deeply connected to transforming and redeeming our powers of imagination and fantasy (See *Tefillin: Wrapped in Majesty* for a detailed exploration).

Phonetically, the word *Cheshvan* sounds similar to the word *Cheshbon* / accounting. If we are struggling to 'find our ground' in order to 'stand up' we can make a *Cheshbon haNefesh* / accounting of the soul in order to bring our spiritual needs, as well as our inner strengths, into awareness and integrity. When our integrity is in alignment on all levels (from Chesed to Yesod), it manifests outwardly as *Chein* / grace, ease, and charisma. Cheshvan begins with a Ches (the word for 'sin') and ends with a Final Nun, thus encoding the whole process of this month's spiritual work and spelling the word *Chein*. As explored earlier, *Chein* is a major theme in the narrative of Noach and the Mabul, both emblematic of various themes and energies in Cheshvan.

In Medieval Europe a large number of terrible decrees were projected upon the Jewish People during the month of Cheshvan (*Bnei Yissaschar*, Cheshvan). Often, it was during this month that harsh taxes (deliberately incorrect Cheshbonos) were imposed upon Jewish communities with the aim of causing them to fall financially. However, our oppressors did not know that the lower we descend into exile, the higher we will ascend into redemption. The lower the Nefilah, the deeper the ground we have as foundation to get up and stand tall. This is how we bring Heaven down to earth, so to speak. Indeed, the prophetic tradition affirms that it is in this month that we will arise together from all our falls, whether spiritual or material, and celebrate the rebuilding of the Temple, speedily in our days (*Yalkut Shimoni*, Melachim 1, Remez 184. *Pesikta Rabsi*, Piska 6). In Cheshvan we learn the hard truth that without falling there is no real flying.

☾

ᘏ
SENSE

*T*HE CONVENTIONAL WORLD IDENTIFIES FIVE SENSES, YET *Sefer Yetzirah* speaks of twelve *Chushim* / senses. In addition to the more commonly understood definition of what comprises our 'senses,' the word *chush* can also mean, 'a sensitive level of perception, understanding, appreciation, and skill' related specifically to a particular biological or cognitive process or function. For example, a 'sense of sleep' is a deep understanding and appreciation of sleep which includes both: a) what sleep represents spiritually, as well as, b) the practical skills and abilities that make one's experience of sleep both peaceful and restorative.

These twelve *Chushim* are also the twelve activities that the Torah describes the Creator performing in the perpetual process of creating and maintaining the world (*Pirush haRavad, Sefer Yetzirah*). As we are created in the Divine image we also possess all twelve *Chushim*, at least in potential.* Every month gives us the ability and strength to expand our vessels (potentials) for a particular *Chush*, along with its corresponding Divine Attributes. When we align and refine our consciousness via these *Chushim*, we can harness the qualities of each month in a most profound and meaningful way.

The 'sense' corresponding to the month of Cheshvan is the sense of smell, the olfactory function. Our sages tell us that the dimension of soul called Neshamah takes particular pleasure in the sense of smell (*Berachos*, 43b). Our body, the outermost dimension of self, receives its sustenance and pleasure from food, whereas the soul, the deepest part of who we are, receives its vitality from smell.

One reason for this is that smell is the only sense that was not damaged or distorted by the Tree of Knowledge of Good and evil, the perception of duality and separation. This is thus the only sense from among our five senses that was not negatively affected by the Snake, the Yetzer haRa. How so?

Smell is the only sense not mentioned in the story of the Garden of Eden: "And the woman saw…" (sight), "and she took…" (touch), "and he ate…" (taste), and "they heard…" (hearing) (*Bereishis*, 3:6-8).

---

* Even if one is blind, for example, he always has the *potential* for sight — it's just that he is currently missing the physical vessels (capacity) for it (*Pirush HaGra*, Hakdamah, *Sefer Yetzirah*). However, the sense of sight is included in the person's Divine image, as it were. Obviously, a physically blind person could have immense vessels for spiritual sight.

All the senses were utilized in the eating or 'internalizing' of the Tree of Duality, besides the sense of smell. Even today, whereas all of our other senses function within the 'Tree' or worldview of duality, our sense of smell remains connected with Gan Eden and the nondual Tree of Life. It can therefore transport us back into Unity-consciousness more directly than any other sense.

The sense of smell is deeply linked with memory, more so than any of our other five senses. Sometimes you can be walking down the street when all of a sudden you get a whiff of a particular smell, a smell similar to one you smelled as a child, for example, the smell of the cottage you vacationed at as a young child, then suddenly, you are completely transported back to that place and the entire memory becomes palpably vivid and immediately present as if decades have vanished. This kind of psychic transport only happens with the sense of smell. Even if you actually went back to the cottage and saw it — if now it smells differently — your memory will not be as strong. This is because smell is free from the obstructions of duality, and it can tap into the unity of the past, present, and future.

Scientifically speaking, smell is rooted in the limbic system of the brain, a most primordial part of the brain. It is a very primal and primitive sense, developed from a time prior to the eating of the Tree of Knowledge, prior to the splitting of the world into conceptual opposites, prior to the world as we know it. Through smell we can return to a unified state of consciousness, as it was before the fall caused by the Snake.

Pleasant aroma in general is related to the concept of Gan Eden. When Yitzchak / Isaac beholds his son Yaakov / Jacob — disguised as his brother Eisav — he says, "See, my son smells like a field that Hashem has blessed" (*Bereishis*, 27: 27). The Medrash explains this to mean that Yaakov smelled like Gan Eden. Thus, when Yaakov walked into the room, an aroma of Gan Eden infused the space. This spiritually pleasant fragrance, when given off by a Tzadik, is connected with purity ("When there was no longer purity among Israel, there was no longer any taste or smell," *Sotah*, 49a. See *Maharsha*, ad loc). Spiritual purity is rooted particularly in purity of physical intimacy (*Eiruvin*, 21b), which is an absence of bodily impurity (*Pri Tzadik*, Sivan 1), a trait mentioned specifically with regard to Yaakov (*Yevamos*, 76a). *Kedushas haBris* / holiness of the covenant, or sexual purity, is also the source of Noach's — and Yoseph's — pleasant trait of Chein. This idea of one's spiritual energy and power being rooted in one's integrity in these areas is referred to as perfecting one's *Midas haYesod* / the personal attribute of intimacy.

Indeed, in the writings of Chazal, Noach is likened to a pleasant fragrance. Rav Yochanan and Reish Lakish argue about whether Noach was only a Tzadik in his generation, or for all other generations as well. In either case, both of these sages compare him to a fragrance. To illustrate their perspective:

Noach was a just man, and perfect in his generation. Rav Yochanan said, "In his generation, but not in other generations." Reish Lakish maintained, " (Even) in his generation — how much more so in other generations." Rav Chanina said, "As an illustration of R. Yochanan's view, to what may this be compared? To a barrel of wine lying in a vault of acid. In its place, its odor is fragrant (by comparison with the acid); elsewhere, its odor will not be fragrant." Rav Oshia said, "As an illustration of Resh Lakish's view, to what may this be compared? To a vial of spikenard oil lying amidst refuse; (if) it is fragrant where it is, how much more so amid spices" (*Sanhedrin*, 108a).

Avraham, whose story we read about in Cheshvan, beginning with the portion of Lech Lecha, is also compared to a pleasant fragrance. Hashem tells Avraham to set out from his homeland saying, he will become great. Says the Medrash (*Bereishis Rabbah*, 39:2), "Avraham was like a closed jar of fragrant myrrh lying in a corner, [as long as he remained where he was] its fragrance did not travel. As soon as it was opened, the scent came out [and spread throughout the world]."

As we mentioned earlier, in Cheshvan we should follow Noach's example of work to perform a Tikkun on any misaligned intimacy and connection between *Mekabel* / receiver and *Mashpia* / giver. Yoseph is the paragon of this Tikkun, as he overcame temptation and was able to live in perfect balance by rectifying his Midas haYesod. It is for this reason that the Torah tells us, when Yoseph was in prison and about to be brought in front of the king of Egypt, "He took a haircut and changed his clothes" (*Bereishis*, 41:14). Based on this verse, the sages ask: Why does he apparently not bathe while in prison? According to the Shach [ad loc], it is because of his holiness; Yoseph did not sweat and therefore did not need to bathe. In a related incident, the wife of the Gra of Vilna once showed her neighbor two garments, one that her husband wore for a few days, and one fresh from being washed. She then pointed out in amazement, "You cannot tell the difference; they both smell perfectly clean." Not only does one's physical (specifically the organ of Yesod) integrity impact their spiritual status and energy, but in turn, one's spiritual integrity impacts their physical body, specifically in the way one smells.

A pleasant aroma alludes to perfect purity, which is connected to the soul, the Luz bone, and to Adam and Chavah's existence in Gan Eden before the Fall. An unpleasant odor alludes to impurity and death. The most intensely foul odor is that which emanates from a lifeless animal, and even worse, a human corpse. Thus bad smells are connected with death and separation, a result of internalizing the Tree of Duality.

Before Adam and Chavah ate from the Tree of Knowledge, their bodies were more brilliant than the light of the sun (*Medrash Rabbah*, Vayikra, 20:2. *Mishlei Rabbah*, at the end. *Tikunei Zohar*, Hakdamah. Note: *Baba Basra*, 58a). They had bodies of *Ohr* / light and they smelled like Gan Eden (Arizal, *Sefer haLikutim*, Bereishis). Once they ate from, and identified with, the Tree of Knowledge, the Torah says, "And Hashem made garments of skin for Adam and his wife and clothed them" (*Bereishis*, 3:21). Instead of being covered by garments of *Ohr* (with an Aleph) / light, they were now covered with garments of *Ohr* (with an Ayin) / skin. After the fall, they were clothed with skin, which is what produces the most foul odor when no longer attached to a living creature (*Kesuvos*, Mishnah 7:10. *Baba Basra*, 16b). Essentially, this means that they lost their inner smell of perfection, of holiness, of purity, the smell of Gan Eden.

A person's smell is connected with their level of physical and spiritual purity (*Sotah*, 49a). Regarding Moshiach, the "perfected human being" connected to the deepest level of soul, it is said, "He shall smell the awe of Hashem" (*Yeshayahu*, 11:3) and, "He shall judge by smell" (*Sanhedrin*, 93b). What you cannot judge by sight, you may still be able to judge by sound. Even more subtle, what you cannot judge by either sight or sound, you may still be able to judge by smell. For instance, we might meet someone for the first time and outwardly they seem friendly, yet in our gut, we 'smell' that this person is up to no good. Or the reverse could be true: we meet someone and outwardly they may appear disheveled and harsh, but our inner sense of smell tells us that they are really a wholesome person on the inside.

Smell is our deepest sense, and as mentioned, is connected directly to our *Neshamah* / innermost soul. King Moshiach himself, who is the 'heart' and 'soul' of *Klal Yisrael* / the People of Israel, uses specifically the sense of smell to judge. Moshiach, by judging with this sense beyond sight and sound, alludes to the fact that his "spiritual judgment," as it were, is rooted in compassion; he will be able to perceive the Divine depths within each person's soul. When we judge ourselves with deep compassionate truth, we empower self-elevation to transform the bitterness in our lives. This is the activation of the spark of Moshiach within each of us, accessible through our power of smell, to connect with the deepest reality, hidden beyond the surface of both sight and sound.

♈

SIGN

ACH MONTH CONTAINS THE ZODIAC INFLUENCE OF A particular constellation, called *Mazal*. A constellation is comprised of a perceivably patterned grouping of visible stars. Today, we count 88 constellations in the night sky. Of all these, one constellation is predominantly visible on the horizon at the beginning of each month.

Each constellation refracts the light of the cosmos different-ly, alternately reflecting times that are more conducive to war, and times that are more conducive for peace, for example (*Yalkut Reuveini, Bereishis,* Oys 56). Additionally, the *Zohar* teaches that each sign can manifest positively or negatively (*Zohar* 3, 282a). In other words, the quality of a constellation can have either a productive or destructive influence in one's life, depending on how we relate to and process its energy. It is important to keep in mind, however, that even if our proclivities are innate or celestially influenced, we still possess the freedom to choose how we respond to the situations that arise in our life. In other words, we have the ability to consciously reflect back what has been projected onto us, even from the stars. For example, a person born under the influence of Mars may have a tendency to be drawn towards blood, but he or she also has the ability to employ this inherent tendency for good as well as ill; such a person could therefore choose to be a violent criminal or a life-saving surgeon (*Shabbos*, 156a).

Due to the prevailing popular belief that the stars exert a kind of fatalistic influence upon world history and human development, we need to repeatedly emphasize that anyone can rise above these influences altogether and be unaffected by them. Despite all the forces and influences in our life — physical and psychological conditions, upbringing, education, environment, financial status, etc. — we always have the freedom to choose. Simply put: we have the choice to live as either the *effect* of our conditions (as passive receivers of what life serves us), or as the *cause* of what comes next, thereby becoming proactive co-creators of our lives. When we begin to live more proactively, the energies of our birth constellation as well as the *Mazal* of each month, function less as positive or negative *influences*, and more as *tools* that can help us climb ever higher into our freedom of being.

The astrological sign of Cheshvan is *Akrav* / the Scorpion, or Scorpio. According to the sages the Akrav is the deadliest of all poisonous creatures. This is reflected in the following teaching: when a person is in the middle of praying the Amidah and a snake winds itself around his feet, he should continue praying; but, if a scorpion gets close to him, he should stop praying [and move] (*Berachos*, 33a). The venom of a scorpion is called cold poison, and the word עקרב / *Akrav* can be split into two: קר / *Kar* / cold and עב / *Av* / dense. The cold, dense power of this venom causes immediate death, as opposed to the 'fiery' venom of a snake.

On an inner psycho-spiritual level, the Kelipah and danger of 'coldness' is much more troubling than the Kelipah of passionate 'heat' or desire for the unholy. If a person is passionate about things of this world and uninterested in spirituality and holiness, it is not so difficult to inspire this person; it is just a matter of redirecting their inherent passion towards the holy. But when a person is cold in general, whether to spirituality or physical pleasures, it is much more difficult and challenging to inspire them to grow. This diagnosis relates to the above teaching regarding an encounter with snakes or scorpions during prayer. If, when praying, the 'hot' passionate venom of the snake — expressed through the distorted fantasies of an overactive imagination — begins to creep up your legs, stay put, continue praying and concentrate even more on your devotions. But if, while you are praying you begin to feel 'attacked' by the cold venom of the scorpion, and you start to experience a feeling of indifference for what you are doing, you must immediately stop praying, pause, breathe, focus and recalibrate.

In other ways, a scorpion is also *similar* to a snake. The word *Akrav* / scorpion is related to the word *Eikev* / heel, and as the Torah says with regard to the Nachash, "And you shall bite him (the human being) on the heel" (*Bereishis*, 3:15). Scorpions too are likely to bite one on the heel or lower extremities. The 'backbone' of a scorpion is bent up and back in a shape similar to the 'bent Nun' at the beginning of the word *Nachash*, but in the opposite fashion. The curvature of a scorpion is dissimilar to a humble downward bow, which breaks the arrogance of ego. The upward bend of a scorpion is an expression of a lifted, inflated ego, which, as we have discussed, eventually causes one's downfall. In Cheshvan we specifically need to counter just these sentiments of inflated ego, which ultimately lead one to depression or cold indifference after inevitable disappointment. As an antidote to the cold venom of the scorpion, present during Cheshvan, we need to learn how to always get up, like a snake, in a wholesome, redemptive way.

Additionally, the word *Akrav* can also be divided into עיקר ב / *Ikar-Beis* / the Main Beis — with the letter Beis alluding to the word *Bayis* / house. The 'Main House' is the rebuilt Temple. Ultimately, as mentioned, it will be during the month of Cheshvan when the Third Holy Temple will be dedicated (See *Bnei Yissaschar*, Cheshvan). In fact, it was also during the month of Cheshvan that the First Beis HaMikdash was completed (*Melachim* 1, 6:38), although it was not dedicated until eleven months later, during the subsequent month of Tishrei. In a sense, then, Cheshvan will be 'compensated' in the Messianic Era for what it missed upon the building and dedication of the First Beis haMikdash

The letters of *Akrav* also spell עקר ב / *Akar Beis* / destroy the Beis, referring to the *Bayis* / House of David. The very first source of rebellion against the Kingdom of the House of David is rooted in the month of Cheshvan. In fact, when Yeravam was accepted as King by ten of the tribes, he proceeded to establish a holiday in the Eighth Month, the month of Cheshvan, designed to draw the people away from Jerusalem (*Melachim* 1, 12:33). Here is the story, briefly:

Yeravam was an officer of King *Shlomo* / Solomon. After King Shlomo's passing, Yeravam demanded that Shlomo's son, King Rechavam rule with more compassion. When Rechavam rejected this, ten of the twelve tribes, excluding the tribes of Yehudah and Binyamin, revolted and declared Yeravam as king of the newly established Northern Kingdom of Israel. To differentiate himself from the House of David and the Beis haMikdash — which was in *Yerushalayim* / Jerusalem within the borders of Yehudah and Binyamin — he tried to establish a 'new' holiday within the eight month, the month we today call Cheshvan. Speaking of Yerav am, the verse [ibid] says that he established holidays "that he had devised מלבו / *m'Libo* / from his heart." In other words, he made up a holiday out of thin air to strengthen his kingdom.

The word *m'Libo* has the same Hebrew letters as מבול / *Mabul* / the Great Flood which began during the month of Cheshvan. It was therefore specifically in the month of Cheshvan, the month of the Mabul and *Bilbul* / confusion and potential downfall of humanity that Yeravam came and tried to *Oker* / uproot the Bayis, to destroy the House of David.

The numerical value of *Akrav* is 372. This is the combined value of the words *David* (14) and *Moshiach* (358). Another name of David is 'Ben Yishai,' Ben (52) plus Yishai (320) also equals 372. Moshiach is the offspring of David who will build the Third Beis haMikdash, repair the brokenness of humanity, and draw righteous people from throughout the entire world to Yerushalayim. Therefore, just as Nachash and Moshiach share the same numerical value, alluding to the fact that Moshiach emerges as a result of rectifying the energy of the Snake, Akrav, the Scorpion, shares a numerical equivalence with David and Moshaich, further alluding to the building of the Third Temple in conjunction with Moshaiach's arrival. This is especially symbolic when one considers how scorpions are so often found among ruins.

On a more mundane and practical level, Scorpio is also a sign of extreme emotional sensitivity, coupled with a potential for obsession. Scorpios can thus be both vengeful and cold, a dangerous combination, making them characteristically slow to forgive. Just as the scorpion's bite is cold, Scorpios can act with a cold temperament. If angry, they can ignore the other person as if they do not exist. If a Scorpio is not your friend, they may very well be your enemy. This cold volatility can lead Scorpios to withdraw from other people, much like the tendency during this month to withdraw into ourselves in 'winter hibernation.'

When, however, the traits of a Scorpio are aligned and elevated, they can be powerfully productive. Their Midah of coldness can be focused into fierce determination to rise up and out from any form of exile or fall. Just as they have a tendency to be slow to forgive, and thus at times fall deeper into despair, they also have the ability to renew themselves, to get up again, no matter how difficult the fall. Scorpios have the intrinsic power to always get up again, and move from the fallen Nun to the final Nun, 'redeeming' themselves and revealing the spark of Moshiach within.

During Cheshvan, many people experience the 'venom of the scorpion,' and suffer from a sense of duality, descent, stumbling, separation, exile or indifference. There might also emerge during this time a sense of 'negative kingship' or disintegration of authentic authority and control — such as the original splintering of the kingdom of David that occurred in Cheshvan. Of course, in the same way that the antidote for a snake bite is contained within the venom itself, the remedy for these particular ailments is also provided during this same month. For instance, the sense of smell contains the antidote to duality, since it induces memory, which unites past, present and future in the Unity that precedes all suffering and exile. The firm ground and upright posture of the final Nun is only found through the humility of the fallen Nun.

To access this antidote, we need to contact and activate our spark of Moshiach within, as it is Moshiach who judges compassionately with his sense of *Re'ach* / smell. The word *Re'ach* has the same letters as *Ru'ach* / spirit. Prior to eating from the Tree of Knowledge, the Spirit of Moshiach was, "hovering over the face of the waters" (*Bereishis*, 1:2. *Rashi*). Water, as discussed earlier, represents a primordial state of unity before creation itself. This suggests that the sense of Re'ach has the power to connect us back to the primordial spirit of non-duality and redemption, back to the Garden of Eden prior to the engagement with the snake.

Adam, meaning simply the human being, is an acronym for *Adam, David, Moshiach* — three incarnations of the same root soul. There is a place within every Adam, every human being, that hovers over the primordial waters prior to the experience of duality. We contact this place within ourselves when we bow in grateful submission to Hashem, and when we act with determination to get up after we fall. When our inner Moshiach is awakened, we can 'smell' the unity and divine awe within ourselves and others. This contributes to the overall collective redemption, when the world will be cleansed of the 'cold venom of the scorpion' and the *Zehumah* / [impassioned] impurity of the Nachash, ushering in the arrival of Moshiach and the building of the Third Temple.

☾

ᴛᴏᵪ
TRIBE

ᴇᴠᴇʀʏ ᴍᴏɴᴛʜ ᴏꜰ ᴛʜᴇ ʏᴇᴀʀ ɪꜱ ᴄᴏɴɴᴇᴄᴛᴇᴅ ᴡɪᴛʜ ᴏɴᴇ of the Twelve Tribes of Israel, the sons of Yaakov (*Sefer Yetzirah*; Medrash, *Osyos Rebbe Akiva*, Dalet). The tribe connected to Cheshvan is Menasheh, named after the older son of Yoseph. Menasheh means, "forgetting." His father Yoseph calls him Menasheh, "because Hashem has made me forget my hardship [while in exile]" (*Bereishis*, 41:51). Menasheh is also connected with separating, or tearing apart (*Rabbeinu Bachya*, Miketz, 44:12). Sometimes, if we have fallen hard, or find ourselves in a difficult situation as Yoseph did, it is more empowering to 'forget' the past and our suffering in order to separate from it and simply stand up again.

When we fall into negative patterns, our sense of *Simchah* / joy in life is deadened; this is the coldness of the scorpion, mentioned above. Genuine joy is further kept at bay if we then continue to ruminate on our failures. In such a case, 'forgetting' the shortcomings of our past can empower us to come alive and joyfully embrace the limitless potential of the present. The word שמחה / *Simchah* contains the same letters that spell the word מחה / *Machah* / to erase. Joy allows us to let go and erase past resentments, whether against ourselves or others. Sometimes the deception of duality has to be forgotten before the truth of unity can be remembered.

In the Torah, up until the introduction of Menasheh and his younger brother Ephrayim, brother-to-brother relationships were especially difficult and even deadly. The first mentioned brother-to-brother relationship was Kayin and Hevel, which ended in fratricide. Then, for various reasons, Yitzchak and Yishmael do not get along; and later Eisav desires to kill his younger twin brother Yaakov for 'stealing' his birthright. The sons of Yaakov also did not get along with their younger brother, Yoseph, and sell him into slavery, even going so far as to fake his death and lie to their father about it for over 20 years.

The first 'healed' relationship between brothers mentioned in the Torah is between Menasheh and Ephrayim. For this, credit is due to the older brother, Menasheh. Why? If we read the text closely we notice that it was always the older brothers (Kayin, Yishmael, Esav, and the older sons of Yaakov) who were envious of their younger brothers, for reasons real or imagined. It was this sense of conflict and constant jockeying for position between brothers which caused the families to fall into strife. Menasheh

had a quality of *Vatranus* / an ability to allow, submit, be humble —
and recognize the greatness and potential in others. This enabled
him to acknowledge the unique gifts and spiritual status of his
younger brother Ephrayim without being jealous of him. He was
therefore able to let go and forget about his own challenges, and
be there to support his little brother. This was, as mentioned, a
Tikkun for all the previously misaligned fraternal relationships in the
Torah, opening up a new path of unity and collaboration for a
higher goal or purpose.

Menasheh also had the Midah of *Hoda'ah* / acknowledgement,
Modim / thanksgiving, and holy submission. Thus his name is
Moshe plus a Nun (the letter of the month). In fact, Moshe is also
called *Menasheh* (with the addition of a Nun) in Tanach (ושבואל בן
גרשם בן מנשה. Baba Basra, 109b. Yerushalmi, *Berachos*, 9:2. *Shoftim*, 18:30. *Divrei
HaYamim* 1, 26:24), and when he passes away, he is buried in *Har Nevo*,
literally, the mountain within which is a Nun.

Additionally, Moshe gives his *Semichah* / transmission of lead-
ership to Yehoshua the son of Nun (literally, a person named Nun)
(*Bamidbar*, 27:23). According to our sages, one's teacher in matters of
Torah is akin to, and some say even more consequential than, one's
biological father (כל המלמד בן חבירו תורה מעלה עליו הכתוב כאילו ילדו) (*Sanhedrin*,
19b). Furthermore, אבידת אביו ואבידת רבו אבידת רבו קודמת. *Baba Metziyah*, 33a). As
Yehoshua's teacher and initiator, Moshe is, allegorically speaking,
also his father. Moshe is thus the *Bechinah* / paradigm of Nun, and
Yehoshua is the 'Son of Nun.'

In the spirit of the bent, regular Nun, Moshe constantly bows
and falls on his face with utter humility in the presence of Hashem.

In line with the final Nun, Moshe also knows how to get up and stand strong as the redeemer of Klal Israel.

Interestingly, if Menasheh represents the fixing of the jealous older sibling (as we had seen generation after generation in the Torah), Moshe represents a new model of younger sibling, sensitive and aware of the volatile feelings of their elders. Moshe humbly showed great respect to his older brother, Aaron — so much so that when he was chosen by Hashem to go take Klal Yisrael out of Egypt, he wanted to defer such awesome responsibility to his older brother, who he said, was a much better public speaker. This initial refusal was only partially due to his skepticism about his own abilities; but was just as much, if not more, an expression of his not wanting to upstage and outshine his older brother Aaron.

According to the Ra'vad [commenting on Sefer Yetzirah and the Siddur of the Ya'vatz], the order of the months follows the order of the tribes' births as recounted in the book of Shemos (*Shemos*, 1:2-5). [This is a different order than the one we predominantly use throughout the *Spiral of Time Series*, which is based on the Arizal.] According to this order, the tribe corresponding to the month of Cheshvan is Dan.

Dan was blessed to be like a snake: "יהי־דן נחש עלי־דרך / Dan shall be a snake on the road" (*Bereishis*, 49:17). Indeed, the symbol of the tribe of Dan is the Nachash.

Eisav engraved the image of a snake on his thigh (*Sefer Tziyoni*, Toldos, p. 44. *Shaloh haKodesh*, Torah shebeKsav, Tzon Yoseph, 12), and it was Chushim, the deaf son of Dan, who fought and decapitated Eisav (*Sotah*, 13a). Chushim (without the Vav) is numerically 358, as is the word *Nachash* / snake. Chushim is thus the one who was able to slay the 'snake' of Eisav. This initiated the very beginning of the redemptive process of Moshiach (which also equals 358), who is the integrated, grounded, upright, rectified energy and imagination of the primordial snake.

Additionally, the word *Dan* literally means, "judge," alluding to the compassionate judgment of Moshiach; connected to the heightened sense of smell, that we strive to emulate in this month.

BODY PART

*E*ACH MONTH IS CONNECTED WITH THE GENERAL ENERGY and particular function of a specific body part. The part of the body corresponding to this month, according to certain versions of Sefer Yetzirah, is the *Dakin* / innards or intestines. This is the part of the digestive system that breaks down and absorbs nutrients. On a deeper level, the function of the *Dakin* is to transform material substances into spirit/energy, as part of the progressive refinement of the material world.

Dakin are also associated with the sense of smell. For example, the animal intestines that were sacrificed on the altar are described in the Torah as giving off a *Rei'ach Nichoach* / pleasant aroma for Hashem. The word *Dakin* is also related to the word *Dak* / to grind.

One of the services of the Temple was the burning of the *Ketores* / Temple incense. The Torah tells us that the Ketores needed to be *Dakah* / thoroughly ground to be offered on the altar (*Shemos*, 30:36. *Vayikira*, 16:12). Rabbi Nassan said (*Kerisus*, 6b), "As one would grind (the incense) another would say, 'Grind thoroughly, thoroughly grind.'" One 'reason' suggested for the inclusion of the incense offering in the Temple services is that it would eradicate the unpleasant odors emanating from the animal offerings (*Rambam, Moreh Nevuchim*, 3:45). On a deeper level, the Zohar writes that the Ketores was offered to transform spiritual unpleasantness into spiritual pleasantness (*Zohar* 2, p.118b).

Cheshvan is a month in which we are pressed to digest the spiritual abundance of Tishrei, in order to fuel and illuminate our souls in the coming winter months. This work of deconstruction and integration requires us to break down and extract the essence of what feeds us on the deepest level. This is the work of the Dakin. Just as the Priests would 'thoroughly grind' 11 different plants to make the Ketores in order to produce a pleasing aroma for Hashem, we too are tasked with transforming our various experiences as well as the world around us into something worth offering up to the Infinite One. If we merit, our very lives will become like the Ketores, and we too will give off a pleasing fragrance for Hashem.

☾

ELEMENT

THERE ARE FOUR PRIMARY ELEMENTS (FUNDAMENTAL building blocks) of creation: fire, air, water, and earth. Each month is associated with one of these four elements. However, it is important to note that while manifesting physically, these elements are also meant to be understood in a much more metaphysical sense, as they represent numerous properties, qualities, and correspondences.*

Cheshvan corresponds to the element of water and, as mentioned, has a primary connection with rain. In fact it is the exact time when autumn rains begin to fall in the Land of Israel (*Ta'anis*, 5a).

---

*For a more in-depth exploration of these elements and their relationship to the Hebrew calendar, please see the introductory volume of this series: *The Spiral of Time: Unraveling the Yearly Cycle*.

The element of water is cold and wet, and this month begins the cold rainy season. The year is shifting into winter, the days are getting colder, and the rains are beginning to fall. Historically, this is the month in which the *Mabul* / Great Flood began. Water is an element that facilitates transition. For example, when the nation of Israel was leaving Egypt and needed to transition out of their prior state of slavery, on all levels, they had to pass through the Sea of Reeds. Similarly, brides and converts immerse in a Mikvah full of water to mark and initiate their transition from one state to another.

The Mabul cleansed the world for 40 days, alluding to the 40 *Sa'ah* (200 gallons) of water required to fill a kosher mikvah. A Mikvah is a place of transition from spiritual blockage and impurity into a new state of aliveness, flow, and conscious purity. Cheshvan is the month of watery transition. You may be experiencing existential impurity, energetic blockage or spiritual fallenness following the month-long 'peak-experience' of Tishrei, but you can always get up. You are more fluid and malleable than you think. Deep within, you possess a wellspring of untarnishable purity. Cheshvan is the time of year we begin to pray for rain, as well as, attempting to tap into our own inner recesses. This is thus a time of both resolve and receptivity.

TORAH PORTIONS

O VER THE COURSE OF A MONTH, 4-5 WEEKLY TORAH portions are read by the community. These individual portions can be combined and viewed as a single unit based on the particular month in which they are most commonly read. Indeed one finds, when viewing the *Parshas* through this calendrical lens, that an astounding array of thematic elements consistent with the spiritual energy of each month is revealed.

Appropriately, based on all that we have covered thus far, the Torah portions most commonly read in Cheshvan focus on themes such as hard work, meeting challenges head-on, picking oneself up after falling, and seeing the presence of Hashem within oneself at every moment and in all situations. All the Parshas are in Bereishis, and they span the stories from Noach to Avraham.

Noach — this Parshah is always read in Cheshvan, synchronizing the narrative of the Mabul with the actual season in which it occurred. The elevation of the lower waters, the descent of the Higher waters, and their ultimate union, symbolically describes our own spiritual work and process during this time: self-generating and awakening from within.

Lech Lecha — this Torah reading begins with the words, "*Lech Lecha...* / Go forth (to you) from your land and from your birthplace and from your father's house, to the land that I will show you" (*Bereishis*, 12:1). The Medrash reads the word *Lecha* / to you, as meaning, "for your own benefit." Avraham is invited to take a journey that is arduous, but also beneficial to him and his cause, allowing him to gather wealth and rise to a status of tremendous influence in the world. The Zohar teaches that *Lecha* is an invitation for Avraham, and for us, to self-actualize and discover the essence of his being; "Go to (become) yourself," actively seek out who you really are. Additionally, *Lecha* can also mean, "by yourself." The journey of 'awakening from below' is difficult, lonely work. It requires focussed *Gevurah* / inner power, and the ability to set boundaries and follow through on commitments in a disciplined and sensitive way.

Vayeira — The memorable words, "*Vayeira* ... And Hashem appeared to him...and he (Avraham) was sitting at the entrance of the tent," begin this week's portion (*Bereishis*, 18:1). What is happening here? Avraham has just circumcised himself at the ripe age of 99 and is recovering from pain in the tent. When Hashem appears to him in his lowly state, Avraham realizes that Hashem is always with him, even when he is 'fallen' — or in pain from his *Bris* / circumcision. So what does he do? He 'gets up' and sits in the heat at the entrance of the tent to seek out and greet guests, despite his pain and discomfort. In this moment Avraham understood that he, and we, must always act in every moment as if Hashem were right there watching us — because He is. Eventually Avraham is elevated to the status of a *Yirah Elokim* / one who is constantly in awe of Hashem (*Ibid*, 22:12). This transformation occurs at the *Akeidah* / binding of Yitzchak, "…He (Avraham) arose and went to the place of which G-d had spoken to him" (22:3). His obedience is an act of 'bowing' in profound humility, as the Torah says, "We will prostrate ourselves and return to you" (22:5).

Chayei Sarah — The literal meaning of *Chayei Sarah* is, "the life of Sarah," although in actuality the portion begins by mentioning her death and burial. This poetic paradox suggests a deeper understanding of life. One can sense life even within death, and elevation within great humility or lowliness. If you feel down or even depressed after the highs of the summer months and Tishrei, you should know that Hashem is here with us even in our lowest points and periods. This knowledge empowers us to live more fully at every moment and with more joy at every juncture of life. We are never alone. We are alive even in death, as no matter what, we always remain connected to the Infinite One.

☾

ༀ

SEASON OF THE YEAR

*T*HE SEASONAL QUALITIES OF EACH MONTH ARE INTERTWINED with the spiritual qualities of that particular time of year. When daylight lasts for longer or shorter periods, different kinds of spiritual light are being revealed on a subtle level as well. The physical experiences of spring are external expressions of the vital pulse of new life and growth emanating during that season. All dark and dank months reflect an energy of corresponding spiritual 'coldness,' stimulating us to seek warmth. People tend to keep to themselves when winter begins and are more outgoing when summer starts. All of these psycho-physical weather patterns reflect deeper realities, as both the earth and mind-body complex are merely reflections of the spiritual realms.

Cheshvan is truly a month of transition. Fall is in full swing and the green leaves of summer are turning brown, perhaps already falling off. Although technically Tishrei is the first of the colder fall months, Tishrei glows with the spiritual warmth of the holidays, so we do not necessarily 'feel the cold' until Cheshvan comes along. Having been positively overwhelmed with the veritable flood of spiritual energies radiating throughout the month of Tishrei, and having been saturated and filled with new life and spiritual vitality, now is the time to return to our homes and our day-to-day work. This retreat and contraction is symbolized by the falling-Nun, discussed at length earlier. Cheshvan is thus an orchestrated period of descent into the *Mar* / bitter (mundane) realms of life. Yet, it is the tasting of these very bitter waters that gives us the opportunity to elevate the *Mar* / bitterness of the mundane and transform it into *Ram* / exaltedness, symbolized by the deeply rooted and upright Nun of redemptive integrity. The literal and figurative cold of this month compels us to 'warm' ourselves by activating and channeling our passions towards positive, righteous, and empowering goals.

Like the earth that was cleansed of self-centered depravity by the Great Flood; we need to allow our deepest inner wellsprings to arise and erase anything that opposes the new reality we have created in Tishrei. As the trees are dropping their leaves, we too need to let self-centered attachments fall away, in order to access and experience the sensation of emptiness and humility that motivates us to transform our bitterness.

Mar is numerically 240, the same value as the word *Safek* / doubt (and *Amalek*). Indeed, since the month of Cheshvan is a time of transition on so many levels, doubts can arise within us. The lofty, holy, connected, inspired feelings you experienced during the High Holidays are suddenly gone, and you may doubt the verity of your experience: were those highs real? Did I really 'connect' on Yom Kippur? Did I really dance on Simchas Torah? Were those lofty visions attainable, or even what I really want? Casting doubt on everything is a natural part of the transitional process.

This is another reason that Cheshvan is connected to the Mabul, the rainy season, and water; because the nature of water is that it does not have a fixed *Tzurah* / form. Water is 'formless' until you pour it into a vessel. On its own, without the tangible boundaries and shape of a vessel, water is undefined — it exists, in a sense, 'prior to Creation.'

This is also the nature of transitions, everything is in flux. In the process of transition you are not the old you, but not yet the new you either. Like flowing water, you do not yet have a defined Tzurah. Between every *Yesh* / some-thing and another (between one Tzurah and another Tzurah), there is a fertile void of formless-ness; this is *Ayin* / no-thing-ness, a *Bitul / nullification* of Tzurah, a liminal space of open-ended fluidity and infinite potential.

In order to transition into, and become a real People, Klal Yisrael needed to pass through the waters at the parting of the Sea of Reeds. They needed to let go of the old mentality of slavery and cynicism, before they could be birthed into the new world of freedom and faith. The parting waters of the sea were like a birth canal ushering them into a new stage of creation. The Song of the Sea, spontaneously self-generated and sung by all of Klal Yisrael on the other side of the Sea of Reeds, was thus the first cry of the proverbial newborn. This is another perfect illustration of our spiritual work in Cheshvan. We too must immerse in and emerge from the cleansing waters, spiritually renewed, and ready for the archetypal journey towards our own personal "promised land" with confidence, gratitude, and humility.

The Mabul lasted 40 days, corresponding to the 40 days of *Yetziras haVelad* / the formation of the Tzurah of a child in the womb. Before 40 days, the child is a pure *Chomer* / unformed substance. Forty days is the amount of time it takes for the newly conceived embryo to assume the full Tzurah of a fetus, a real child. Thus, the purity of the Generation of the Flood was created when they finally emerged from the Ark with a new Tzurah. For 39 days there was a total *Bitul* of their negative, impure Tzurah. Then, after the 40th day, a new Tzurah emerges from the Ayin, from the *Mar* / bitter (also *Mar* / drops of rainwater). What emerged from the ark was a *Beriah Chadashah* / a totally new creation. This is the process of the Mikvah of the Mabul. Similarly, in Cheshvan we enter into a place of 'water,' of fluidity and even *Safek* / doubt, before we can transition to *Ram* / exaltated elevation and uprightness.

ᔤ

THE HOLIDAYS
OF THE MONTH

"FOR EVERYTHING THERE IS AN APPOINTED TIME" (*KOHE-LES*, 3:1). In other words, everything happens according to Divine timing (Rebbe RaYatz, *Sefer haMa'amorim*, tof-shin-aleph, p. 59). Our Sages tell us that when we left Egypt, it was the appointed time for such liberation. This means that not only did it occur in its historically appropriate time, but also at the right time of year — the season best suited for this expression of Redemption (*Mechilta deRabbi Yishmael*, Bo, 16, on the verse in Tehillim, 68:7. *Rashi*, Sotah, 2a). This is the same principle behind every Yom Tov. The narrative and observance of each celebration or fast reflects and refracts the light of the natural world through its spiritual lens.

Furthermore, in the months that contain a *Yom Tov* / holiday, that Yom Tov embodies and encapsulates the energy of the entire month in condensed form. Similarly, in a month that does not have a major holiday or observance, that absence is also an expression of the unique energy of the month.

And in fact, Cheshvan is just such a month that possesses no significant holidays or observances. Yet, interestingly, as mentioned, following the splintering apart of the kingdom of the House of David in ancient Israel, Yeravam attempted to create his own holiday in the month of Cheshvan, since it was devoid of holidays. In a positive context, we too need to establish holy days or 'awakenings from below' in this month; lest we end up falling too deep, down into the formless 'waters' of this month. We thus need to ensure that every 'mundane' day is vested with meaning and purpose. That our every ordinary moment becomes inwardly extraordinary.

In this spirit, there are various historical events in Cheshvan that can be characterized as relating to a type of *awakening from below*, self-empowerment, or living from the inside-out; further testifying to the signature quality of this month:

- On the Seventh of Cheshvan each year, people in Israel begin praying for rain. This is because during the Second Temple era, this date is when the last travelers would arrive home after spending Sukkos in Yerushalayim. Rain any earlier would have impeded their travels (Mishnah, *Ta'anis* 10a. *Shulchan Aruch*, Orach Chayim, 117:1). Therefore, on this day in Cheshvan, the entire community has returned to a normal routine. Rain, in contrast to dew, is dependent on our actions. Although we also pray for dew each spring, dew "is never withheld" (*Ta'anis*, 3a). Whether we deserve it or not the earth is always blessed with dew. Rain, on the other hand is dependent on our deeds and prayers, in other words, our degree of *awakening from below*.

- When vegetation was created, the Torah says, "And all the wild plants had not yet sprouted, because Hashem had not brought rain on the earth and there was no human being to work the ground" (*Bereishis*, 2:5). What is the connection between "no human being to work the earth" and rain? Rashi (ad loc) explains, the reason there were no rains yet was precisely because "there was no human being," and therefore, no one present to make efforts to 'awaken' or merit the rain. Through our own actions, as it were, we generate rain; it is an outward manifestation of our state of self-generation.-

On the 17th of Cheshvan the rains of the Mabul began, lasting 40 days. On the 27th of Cheshvan, one year and 10 days later, Noach and his family left the *Teivah* / ark after it rested atop Mount Ararat. Thus the full cycle of cleansing, clearing, and bridging the upper and lower waters begins and ends in Cheshvan.

- During this month the *Malchus Beis David* / Monarchy of the House of David fractured and separated, and there was a rebellion against King Shlomo's son (*Melachim* 1, 12:33. *Melachim* 2, 17:21). Perhaps the root reason for wanting to revolt was justified, as they requested that their new king judge with compassion. An even deeper motivation was their desire to self-generate and live justly with no need for a king at all. This more radical reason is aligned with the admonition of the Prophet *Shemuel* / Samuel when the people originally asked for a king. In either case, the point is that there is a type of rebelliousness, a drive and desire to live autonomously from the inside-out, that arises in Cheshvan, although this desire needs to be properly focused and directed, so it will be productive rather than destructive.

For, as we can plainly see, there were real repercussions to this splintering of the House of David. Meta-historically, it was a breaking apart of rectified rulership and true justice, which gave rise to various manifestations of negative and unjust rulerships and corruption of the law. For this reason, especially during the Medieval period, many corrupt and negative 'judgments' and laws, such as high and punishing taxes, were imposed upon Klal Yisrael. These decrees were often announced or put into action during the month of Cheshvan, and they often led to an increase of persecutions and humiliations during this time (Rabbi Mendel of Rimanov. See: *Bnei Yissaschar*, Cheshvan, 1. *Agra d'Pirka*, 121. *Sheim MeShemuel*, Noach).

- In the times of Moshiach the Third Beis haMikdash will be dedicated in this month because a) it was originally completed in this month, b) it will be a Tikkun for the division of the monarchy, and because this is the month that c) we most passionately activate our inner Moshiach, the deepest resource of our soul, by mustering the strength to continue getting up after we have fallen. This practice and experience of 'awakening from below' is key to transform the fallen Nachash (bent Nun) into the upright Nachash (final Nun).

We must thus strive during Cheshvan to access our inner power to get up again and again, until the outer and Ultimate Redemption is revealed as a result of our labors.

The deepest *Koach / power* of the Neshamah, this dormant mark of the inner Moshiach, once activated, can push us to get up, and get up again, to never give up, and to finally overcome the current *Galus / exile* of history. Every time we get up and regain our true stature, we hasten the arrival of the *Moshiach haKelali /* the universal Moshiach.

The Yid haKodesh once asked Rebbe Simcha Bunim to tell him what kinds of things he heard people saying in the marketplace. Reb Bunim responded that he heard them saying, "To lose money is not so bad, but when you lose courage, you lose everything."

Yes, we may sometimes fall, and maybe hard even, but let us always remember that our true greatness comes from the way we pick ourselves up after we have fallen. Every obstacle is another opportunity!

☾

❧ SUMMARY OF CHESHVAN

*I*N THE MONTH OF CHESHVAN WE DESCEND FROM THE SPIRI-
TUAL and psychological highs of Tishrei into a period without the influx of light from any official **holidays**. The **season**,
too, is transitioning into a darker and colder time of year. The cold
corresponds to the behavior of the scorpion, which is Scorpio, the
sign of the month. All of this stimulates a need to self-generate
warmth from within, to 'awaken from below' and learn to get up
when we are falling, as suggested by the **Torah portions** of the
month. The **letter** Nun also describes this process of self-generated
elevation, from the 'fallen' regular Nun to the 'standing' final Nun,
as does this month's **letter sequence of Hashem's name**.

When we stand up after having fallen, we sweeten our *Mar /* bitterness, as suggested by the transformation of the **name of the month**, from Mar Cheshvan to Ram Cheshvan. Relatedly, the Torah **verse** of the month also contains the word *D'vash /* honey, alluding to the work of sweetening our lives, that is the focus of this month. The act of standing up after falling also gives rise to a *Re'ach Nicho'ach /* pleasant aroma, enjoyed by the Creator — smell being the **sense** of the month.

The **element** of water has the formless quality that we need to pass through in order to recreate ourselves. We also need to employ the qualities of the **body part** of the month, the *Dakin /* intestines, which function to convert matter into spirit. And finally, we need to summon the humility of Menasheh, for whom the **tribe** of the month is named.

12 DIMENSIONS OF CHESHVAN	
Sequence of Hashem's Name	Vav-Hei-Hei-Yud (descriptive of an *awakening from below*)
Torah Verse	Devarim, 26:15-16: "...Honey. Hashem (commands you) today...." (suggestive of sweetening bitterness)
Letter	Nun — the regular Nun is falling or collapsed, the final Nun stands upright.
Month Name	The Eighth Month (relating to transcending nature, and to Moshiach); *Bul*, from *Balah /* wither. (Mar/Ram) Cheshvan.
Sense	*Re'ach /* smell
Zodiac	*Akrav /* Scorpio
Tribe	Menasheh (son of Yoseph)

Body Part	*Dakin* / intestines
Element	Water (suggestive of rain)
Parshios	Noach through Chayei Sarah (Meeting challenges, picking oneself up after falling)
Season	Fall (month of seasonal transition)
Holiday	No official holidays. Historical creation of a holiday by Yeravam demonstrates *awakening from below.*

~ PRACTICE

THINKING ABOUT TRANSITIONS

As the season is changing and it's getting colder, and as we are transitioning into the winter, Cheshvan is a perfect time to think about transitions in general, and especially about the continuous changes in our lives.

Life is forever changing. Every day that we live we are getting older. We are actually, if you think about it, transitioning continually, moment by moment. Broadly speaking, we move from being a child to an adult, and with Hashem's help, to a spouse, a parent and grandparent. Many of the people in our lives, from when we were children, start passing away as we age. Change is really the only constant in life.

During Cheshvan, it's part of our spiritual work to take the time and consider, how do we navigate through the transitions of our lives? Perhaps we experienced the loss of a loved one or the birth of a child, or a change in our job over the last year. Think about which changes were of your own doing and which were circumstantial. How did you respond to the challenges that presented themselves? When dramatic change occurs in your life, do you feel 'knocked down'? Does a time of doubt or 'formlessness' cause you to collapse, even just subtly? If so, what do you do, or can you do, to empower yourself, find your balance, and pick yourself back up? These are the guiding questions of Cheshvan.

DON'T GIVE UP, JUST GIVE!

We should never give up or despair. We should never let our doubts drag us down and drown us in the Ayin of our transitional periods.

No matter how difficult the past, each day presents us with new possibilities for positive change. Often the best way to get up, after you have fallen into doubt or depression, is to stop focusing on yourself and try to help another who is in need.

When a person is feeling down he can harbor an ironic, almost perverse, preoccupation with himself. The very act of giving to another, reaching out to someone outside oneself, is psychically cleansing and spiritually clarifying as to what really matters. Not only does it allow you to focus on something other than your own depression, by helping an other, your life begins to have greater meaning again. The awareness that you are needed, valuable, that you matter to others, can help alleviate the self-centered agony of depression.

A grandson of one of the great Chassidic Rebbes once fell into a funk. When they asked him why, he said it was because of the Aleph Beis. "Aleph stands for the first letter of the word *Anochi* / I, and Beis stands for the first letter of the word *Bereishis* / in the beginning. The source of my depression," he said, "is that my 'I' is always present, in every beginning. Everything always starts with my 'I.'"

A person who is suffering from emotional depression (as opposed to clinical depression, which is another issue) needs to generate a new focal point. In such a situation, there is usually a preoccupation with 'how I am feeling,' and paradoxically, the more a person thinks about himself, the deeper he sinks. To help a person out of their spiritual or emotional fall, direct their focus towards someone else and their needs. Help them make a transition from egocentricity to other-centricity.

Doing something for someone else has the power to sweeten our own predicament and transform our *Mar* / bitterness into sweetness. In the Land of Israel there are two seas that are linked, the Galilee, which is sweet and drinkable, and the Dead Sea, which is bitter and lifeless. Both bodies of water originate in the Golan. The same water flows from the Golan into the Galilee and then collects in the Dead Sea. The Galilee gives of its waters, and its waters are characteristically sweet. The Dead Sea does not give, it stubbornly hordes and focuses on the water it has, its waters gather, cease flowing and become bitter. This metaphor is self-explanatory. By offering ourselves to others, we sweeten our own waters.

KAVANAH
MINDFUL INTENTION:

Hishtavus / Equanimity

In Cheshvan we can be emotionally affected by the significant changes in the physical and spiritual climates. Because of this, many people tend to experience an amplified desire to be alone and retreat from others, as if to hibernate. This often leads to increased feelings of melancholy and isolation. To counter these internal feelings, as well as the external climatic influences, we can tap into the mindstate of *Hishtavus* / equanimity. It is through *Hishtavus* that we will learn to support ourselves, generate our own buoyancy from within, and become less dependent on the outside world for our happiness and sense of self-worth. By generating our own happiness, we save ourselves and others, from descending deeper and deeper into the pit of self-inflicted suffering.

To live with Hishtavus is to live an equanimous, balanced life; unaffected by outside influences. It is not 'stoicism' in the pessimistic or nihilistic sense. It is not to somehow be immune to life's ups and downs or insensitive to others. *Hishtavus is the sensation that everything that is happening in the moment is exactly how it should be.*

Hishtavus is being rooted firmly within yourself, and proactively emanating outward, rather than the other way around. People are generally affected by the opinions of the society which surrounds them; and gain their sense of self-worth in relation to second-hand observations of others. Hishtavus is the state in which everything is understood to be equal, and you are therefore unaffected by the praise or apparent scorn of others.

The source of human suffering is the *Cheit* of eating from the Tree of Knowledge. When Hashem tells Adam and Chava not to eat from this specific tree, they were meant to understand that their choices have consequences. That they do not need to let the voice of the snake, or any external stimulus, dictate their mood or validate their actions. They were supposed to practice Hishtavus, and remain rooted in what they knew to be true, regardless of the opinions of others.

After the fall from Edenic consciousness, Hashem asks Adam, 'What happened?' He replies, "The woman that You gave me gave it to me" (*Bereishis*, 3:12). By avoiding taking responsibility for his own choice, Adam falls even further from Hishtavus. Hashem then turns to Chavah, and she too replies, "The Snake convinced me" (3:13). They are banished from Eden, and they each receive a curse for betraying their inner truth.

The curse of Chavah is that the *Itzavon* / suffering or hardship of child-labor will be amplified. By extension, she will also experience enhanced *Tzar Gidul Banim* / the suffering involved in raising children. The curse on Adam is that he will only eat his bread *b'Itzavon* / in grief and hardship. In other words, he will find it extremely difficult to make a living.

As mentioned earlier in regards to Noach, Rashi compares *Itzavon* to when a person plants legume seeds and expects legumes to sprout, yet thorns come up instead. When we invest in acquiring happiness from the outside world, suffering sprouts up in its place. When we blame other people or conditions for our own problems, we collapse deeper into this very experience of *Itzavon*. When *Itzavon* festers, it becomes a source for *Atzvus* / depression.

"And Hashem said, 'Let us make the human in Our image, according to Our likeness; and let them have dominion over the fish of the sea...'" (*Bereishis* 1:26). The words *vaYirdu b'Dagas haYam* / and you will have dominion over the fish of the sea.... allude to *vaYardu* / and you will decline, descend, or fail. This is a natural part of life. However, when humanity falls and does not apply equanimity, but instead continues to sink deeper and deeper as they grasp for more of the same emptiness, the whole of creation can be brought down as well. In fact, when the image and semblance of the Creator becomes corrupted in the human heart, it is only a matter of time before the earth too is, "filled with corruption." This is because the entire earth is included within the human heart, which is why the earth itself was also cursed as a result of Adam and Chava's eating from the Tree of Knowledge. This emphasizes how important our actions and awareness of Hishtavus is.

Hishtavus is *the* Tikkun for Itzavon, the undoing of the effects of the original *Cheit* of Adam and Chava. Noach made strides towards this rectification, but in the end, ultimately failed. How? According to some Medrashim, the forbidden fruit eaten by Adam and Chava was actually the grape, and specifically wine. To address this, immediately after coming out of the *Teivah* / Ark, Noach's first act was to plant a vineyard. He wanted to drink wine in a holy manner, and with a redemptive positivity, that would undo the *Cheit*. Yet, he failed in this attempt when he became subtly dependent on the outer circumstances of life for his sense of happiness. When the world around him did not provide him with the positivity that he needed, he sought relief in getting drunk. He dropped his Hishtavus, and fell down even deeper.

To undo the *Cheit* and return ourselves, and humanity, to Edenic consciousness, we must take responsibility for our own experiences of life, and refrain from blaming others or external conditions for our suffering. In other words, We must practice Hishtavus — especially after we ourselves have fallen. For without this awareness, the very fact that we have fallen will only bring us down more, as we become entangled in a self-fulfilling prophecy of negativity.

One method for increasing Hishtavus is to meditate on the verse, *Shivisi Hashem leNegdi Tamid* / I have placed Hashem in front of me, always (*Tehilim*,16:8). The simple meaning of these words is an affirmation of the fact that we are in Hashem's presence at all times (*Shulchan Aruch*, Orach Chayim, 1:1). Another (hyper)-literal read of this verse is, 'I place the four letters of Hashem's Name, Yud-Hei-Vav-Hei (י-ה-ו-ה), in front of my mind's eye at all times.' One may practice this meditation at anytime, anywhere, by simply visualizing these four letters as they appear in black ink on parchment (*Mearas Einayim*, Parshas Ekev. *Maggid Mesharim*, Parshas Miketz. Parshas Vayikra. *Sha'ar Ruach haKodesh*, Derush 1. *Sha'arei Kedusha* 3, Sha'ar 4. *Likutei Torah*, Ta'amei haMitzvos, p. 132).

Alternatively, Rabbi Yitzchak of Acco (*Meiras Einayim*, Ekev) writes that the word *Shivisi* has the same letters as the word *Shav* / equal, and therefore *Shivisi* means *Hishtavus* / equanimity; thereby rendering the phase as more psychologically, 'I have attained equanimity through the constant awareness of being in Hashem's Presence.' Interestingly, Rabbi Yitzchak tells a related story about a student who once approached a spiritual master and asked him to teach secret wisdom. The teacher, in classic fashion, responded to this request with a question of his own. He asked him, "Have you attained equanimity?" The student was thrown off guard and asked the master to clarify the meaning of this pointed question. "Well," replied the master, "do you feel happy when you are praised, or sad when you are derided?" The student responded, "Yes, master, I do. I feel good when I am complimented, and I feel bad when I am criticized." The teacher immediately dismissed him and told him to come back when he achieved equanimity.

Attaining Hishtavus takes patience, much practice, and perseverance. It will also inevitably involve numerous 'failures,' falling from the heights of your ideal. But this is just part of the program. We must also apply Hishtavus to any sense of failure, even within the process of acquiring Hishtavus itself. This equanimity, in the face of a 'lack of equanimity,' will give us the clarity and strength of character to continuously get up and keep striving.

Practically, it is best to focus on Hishtavus for specific/circumscribed periods of time, so that we do not become overly stoic or indifferent to our environment. The delicate balance of a mature state of Hishtavus includes being unaffected by other people's energy, while still being available and responsive to their needs in a moment of real encounter. Actually, if you are 'unaffected' to the right degree, you can even be *more* available to others. This is because our emotionally-charged reactions, and self-validating thoughts, often tend to obscure others' needs and get in the way of the light of the person with whom we are interacting with. Hishtavus keeps you from being dragged down into, and limited by, those self-centered reactions and thoughts. This ultimately allows for a greater level of connection and compassion, since when you remove your ego from the interpersonal equation, you can receive the other directly.

Your Hishtavus should extend to all areas of your life. If, when you wake up in the morning and it is raining outside, you let these dreary conditions dictate how you are going to experience your day, you are falling from Hishtavus. If you wake up in the morning and the sun is shining, and because of this you decide you will have a good day, you are still allowing the external world to dictate your experience. If you just had good coffee and this is what is making you feel good — or if your coffee was too watery and because of this you are in a lousy mood, it is no different than being deflated by other people's opinions. In each of these cases, the external world, not your inner compass, is dictating and directing your emotions and actions. You are, in those moments, submitting to the voice of the proverbial snake. To live from a place of Hishtavus is to live from the inside-out; when you root yourself and take a stand in your chosen inner-state of mind and being, nothing outside of you can deceive or distract you from your true stature.

When you live with Hishtavus, you sense that life is as it should be, always perfect and whole. Whether people praise or scorn you, whether you are hungry or full, whether you are succeeding financially or not, it is all essentially equal. It is not that you become indifferent; a compliment is still a compliment and tasty foods are still tasty; they (or their opposite) just don't throw you off kilter. You remain rooted in a deeper foundation that allows you to maintain a state of emotional equilibrium amid all of life's ups and downs. In addition to enhancing our own well-being, Hishtavus enables us to be even more clear-headed and effective in our attempts to connect with, and help, others. Hishtavus allows us to fix what is broken in the world.

To practice and develop a state of Hishtavus, begin by taking a few moments every day, preferably in the morning, for objective introspection. Earnestly ask yourself questions such as the following:

From where do I gain my sense of self-worth?

Is my self-worth dependent on other people's opinions of me?

Do I need (or desire) other people's praise to feel good about myself?

Do I feel good about myself when other people praise me, and feel bad about myself when others criticize me?

Can I gain my self-confidence from within and 'self-generate' my experience of life?

Now extend these questions outside the realm of the interpersonal:

Do I need the sun to shine in order to feel happy?

When it is rainy or cloudy, do I feel down?

Do I need specific foods or drinks or clothes to be content?

Can I 'self-generate' and choose from within to be in a good mood?

While Hishtavus is certainly important throughout the entire year — it is especially apropos during Cheshvan, a month of seasonal changes and spiritual transitions, a month full of rain and lacking the light of any holidays. Such a time is the ideal proving ground for the development of Hishtavus.

᪂

ESSAYS ON RAIN*

WHAT IS RAIN?

C HESHVAN IS THE OFFICIAL BEGINNING OF THE RAINY SEASON in the Land of Israel. As we have explored throughout the course of this text, this seasonal phenomenon has numerous symbolic, spiritual, environmental, and experiential implications. However, we have yet to address the most basic question: what is rain?

Of course we know the most primary material definition of rain, but what is rain on a deeper level, and what could or should our relationship to it be? On one level, rain is natural and seemingly commonplace, and yet, there is a full Talmudic tractate in *Ta'anis* which discusses various aspects of the physical and spiritual significance of rain.

---

* The following two essays are transcriptions of a *Shiur* / lecture given by Rav Pinson in The IYYUN Kolel (Cheshvan, Ayin-Hei). Each Talmid has internalized and written in their own unique way. Essay one was composed by Reb Eden Pearlstein and essay two by Reb Mattisyahu Brown.

According to Chazal there are many wonderful ways to understand the nature of rain. For instance, the Gemara in *Ta'anis* says,
"גדול יום הגשמים מתחיית המתים / the day of rain is greater than the
resurrection of the dead." In *Talmud Bavli*, rain is compared to, "the
day the Torah was given" (*Ta'anis*, 7a), and the *Yerushalmi* (*Ta'anis*, 1:1)
says that, "rain is חיים לעולם / eternal life, or the life of the world."
It is clear from these, and other extended ruminations on the nature
of rain throughout Torah and Chazal, that the sages understood
that there was more to rain than its physical manifestation. There
is in fact a qualitative dimension to rain that is deeply connected
to, and even reflective of, our own state of spiritual alignment and
social integrity.

In this essay, we will attempt to gain a deeper sense of the essence of rain, as well as its significance for our experience of life
on every level. We will begin by briefly introducing a handful of
relevant ideas and images related to rain, culled from a diverse body
of texts and genres of Torah thought, which we will then revisit
and synthesize at the end of our inquiry.

Earth - Human - Heaven

For starters, it is relevant to mention in relation to much of what
we have spoken about in the previous pages, that the Zohar frames
the issue of rain in a relational context of giving and receiving; the
rain is considered the giving/masculine principle (the seed) and the
earth is considered the receiving/feminine principle (the womb)
(See also *Yerushalmi*, Berachos, 9:2). Or, in the language of the Gemara,
" מיטרא בעלה דארעא / Rain is the husband of the earth" (*Ta'anis*, 6b).
This is wholly consistent with what we have discussed previously

regarding the generation of Noach and the waters of the Great Flood. The overall quantity and quality of rain at any point in time is representative of the current state of balance and alignment, or lack thereof, between the heavens and the earth. But where does humanity, where do we, factor into this equation?

As in all things, the primary source for our understanding of rain is to be found in the Torah. Following the description of the Six Days of Creation, the Torah says that vegetation had not yet sprouted upon the earth because it had not rained, as there was no human to work the land. Famously, Rashi (*Bereishis*, 2:5) referencing various Medrashim (*Chulin*, 60b. *Medrash Rabbah*, Bereishis, 13:8) comments, "rain had not yet fallen upon the earth because there was still no human to pray for rain." We will continue to explore the many depths of meaning contained within this comment, but for now, suffice it to say that on some level Rashi is stressing the human role in mediating this elemental relationship between the heavens and the earth.

The Arizal, commenting on this same verse, says that essentially there was no *Tzemach* / vegetation on the earth because, "the rain of Beriah did reach the earth, since there was no man from the world of Yetzirah." In simpler language, this means that the waters from *Olam haBeriah* (we'll understand what this means in a moment) had not yet irrigated the earth because there was no *Memutzah* / intermediary between the earth (which is *Asiyah,* physicality), and the heavens (which is *Beriah,* spirituality). In other words, there was no *Yetzirah* / formation between the world of *Beriah* / conception and *Asiyah* / actualization; there was no connecting agent (or consciousness) between raw potential and tangible manifestation.

The human being is that connectivity, the connecting pipe, so to speak, that ties the world of potential and the world of the actual together in one cohesive framework. Therefore there was no rain until the human being was created.

However, if you look closely at the writing of the Arizal, it does not simply say that 'there was no rain,' what he says is that there was no rain from the world of Beriah. So, there was rain from the world of Asiyah, but no rain from the world of Beriah? What does this mean practically? What is the difference between rain from the world of Asiyah and rain from the world of Beriah?

Remembering & Requesting the Rains

The section of the Gemara in *Ta'anis* which focuses on rain, starts off by introducing a *Machlokes* / sacred disagreement between Rabbi Eliezer and Rabbi Yehoshua; "מאימתי מזכירין גבורות גשמים / from when do we begin mentioning rain [in the second blessing of the Amidah]?" This is obviously a technical Halachic question pertaining to our liturgical calendar. However, as with all things Torah related, there are worlds of deeper significance encoded into this debate that we will continue to excavate.

For starters, it is important to point out that there are two different blessings in the Amidah in which we mention rain, beginning in the fall season. The first is mentioned above, we 'remember the rains' in the second blessing, which we begin reciting at the end of Sukkos. The second is a petitionary prayer for rain in the ninth blessing of the Amidah. The former is an act of *Hazkaras* / remembrance and the latter is a real *She'ila* / request.

When do we begin to request rain? One opinion, offered in *Ta'anis*, is the third day of Cheshvan. The second opinion, which is how we hold today, is offered by Rav Gamliel; he says that in Israel we begin praying for rain on the seventh of Cheshvan, 15 days after the end of Yom Tov (*Ta'anis*, 10a). The logic behind this ruling is that it would take a maximum of 15 days for the last person, who came to Yerushalayim for the Sukkos festival, to return home.

Obviously rains are beneficial for the earth and crops, but not so much for travelers at the mercy of the elements. In other words, during Sukkos (which in many ways is all about stirring up and preparing for rain) we begin to 'remember' the rains, and specifically to marvel at Hashem's power to apportion them. Yet it is not until the 7th of Cheshvan, after all holiday pilgrims have safely returned home, that we actually begin to directly petition Hashem to bring the rains. This liturgical choreography of rain-related prayers is a beautiful example of the ways in which the power of the heavens, the cycles of the earth, and the needs of humanity are all interwoven with such heightened sensitivity within Torah and Chazal.

Two Types of Rain: Geshem and Matar

In addition to the two kinds of rain-related prayers discussed above, there are also two different words we use to describe two distinct categories or conceptions of rain. When you remember the rains in the second blessing, you say, "who circulates the winds and brings down *Geshem* / the rains." What is the word you use for rain in this context? *Geshem*. And when you are petitioning

HaKadosh Baruch Hu for rain in the ninth blessing, what is the word that you use? *Matar*. Why, when you're 'remembering' rain, do you say *Geshem*, and when you are asking for rain, you say *Matar*? What is the difference between these two different types of rain?

Rabbeinu Bachya (*Devarim*, 11:17) states that, "ואותו שהוא ממי אוקיאנוס אינו נקרא מטר אלא גשם / the lower waters, those of the ocean, are called Geshem, not Matar." Geshem comes from the word *Gashmiyus* / physicality or materiality, as he explains. Alternatively, he states that, "ואותו שהוא ממים העליונים נקרא בשם שניהם בלשון מטר ובלשון גשם / and the rain from the upper waters are referred to by both names, Matar and Geshem." The lower waters (Geshem) are thus understood as exclusively physical (Gashmiyus), while the upper waters are inclusive of the material level (Geshem) as well as something else yet to be described (Matar).

Similarly, the Malbim explains the difference between Geshem and Matar, "*Geshem hu Tiv'i* / Geshem is natural," and, "*Matar hu Hashgochi* / Matar is providential." Geshem and the lower waters are considered 'natural' waters, while Matar and the upper waters are what we can call 'intentional' or spiritual waters.

Without getting too lost in the details and finer points of these definitions (of which there are certainly many), the relevant point for us is that rain inspires two distinct types of prayerful expression. On one hand it inspires a type of wonder-filled praise, while on the other hand it elicits a form of direct petition. This double mentioning is unique to rain in the context of our *Davening* / prayers. You do not, for example, see this in relation to *Refuah* / healing. You don't *Mazkir* / remember that Hashem is a *Rofei Chal Basar* /

healer of all flesh in one blessing, and then make a request for such healing in a separate Tefilah.

Rain therefore seems to have some type of dual nature that inspires us to relate to it on different levels. But what is it exactly in the nature of rain that compels these two types of expressions? What is rain?

Rain as Chesed, Rain as Gevurah

To answer this question, we must first recognize that there are two phenomenological aspects of rain. There is the actual *Shefa* / flow of rain itself coming down into this world, and then there is the *Oifen haShefa* / way it comes down — this includes the where, when, and how much. There is thus the 'what' of rain, and the 'how' of rain.

On one hand rain represents a unified flow of abundance. In the Gemara, when it discusses *Choni Hama'agal*, the only sage who could effectively *Daven* / pray for rain on behalf of the people, it says that rain is called *Rov Tovah* / a lot of good or good for the multitudes (*Ta'anis*, 23a). Rain gives life, it is *Mechayeh Meis-im* / resurrecting the dead, it's enlivening the plants, it brings about a re-emergence of what is beneath the dust. The world is dead and the rain comes and enlivens it, it impregnates it, rain allows the earth to give birth. Chazal even go so far as to compare a day of rain to the day the world was created (*Ta'anis*, 7b). So, on the one hand, there is an inherent *Chiyus* / enlivening energy related to rain, which is a *Chesed* / unimpeded kindness, a unified flow that has a general function in the structure of creation.

On the other hand the sages refer to *rain as* גבורות גשמים /
Gevuros Geshamim / rains of Gevurah or "might of the rains" (*Ta'anis,*
2a). Gevurah implies that rain is not just a general, unified flow, a
Chesed; it is also very particular, it is detailed, discerning. Hashem
says to Iyov, "הרבה טיפין בראתי בעבים וכל טיפה וטיפה בראתי לה דפוס בפני
עצמה / I have created many different raindrops and every single
raindrop has its own particular mold." Every single raindrop is different and if one raindrop would be too similar to another one, the
whole world would be destroyed.

So then, is rain a collective entity, 'the rain' as it were, or is
it comprised of countless individual raindrops? In quantum
terminology, we could translate this question as: is rain a wave
(chesed) or a particle (gevurah)? Is rain a general phenomenon in
the natural process of the world, or is it an answer to our personal
prayers? Furthermore, Does Hashem only relate to the world as an
impersonal generality, or does Hashem relate in a personal way to
each one of His creations?

Conceptually, rain contains and combines both the qualities of
a *Rov Tovah,* a unified flow of Chesed for the general collective,
as well as being comprised of *peratim* / individual parts or details,
representing Gevurah and the needs and experiences of individuals. Which is why the sages instituted that we both 'remember'
the rains and pray for them in our daily liturgy. Rain allows us to
recognize the Creator in nature and creation in general, as well
as in the particular details of our personal lives. Rain thus reveals
multiple aspects of Hashem: the Universal Creator and Sustainer
of the worlds, and the indwelling Presence that we can pray and
cry out and relate to.

Does Rain come from Above or Below?

Returning to our Gemara in *Ta'anis* we find another debate between Rabbi Eliezer and Rabbi Yehoshua concerning the source and nature of rain. Rabbi Eliezer says,"כל העולם כולו ממימי אוקיינוס הוא שותה / the entire world receives its waters from the *Okyanus* / the lower waters of the ocean, as it says in the verse, 'and [the rains] rose up from the earth.'" Rabbi Yehoshua says, no, "כל העולם כולו ממים העליונים הוא שותה / all the world receives its water from the Upper Waters (*Ta'anis*, 9b).

Essentially Rabbi Eliezer is claiming that everything comes from its source in nature; this is how he interprets the verse, "and [the rains] rose up from the earth." [I.e. rain appears as a result of the waters of the world evaporating from below, and rising above to form clouds, which then rain down. This is the natural water-cycle of our planet earth.] Rabbi Yehoshua, on the other hand, claims that rain comes from the higher waters, from the heavens and the earth, from Tefilah as well as weather patterns.

Interestingly, Rabbi Eliezer and Rabbi Yehoshua are the same sages who famously argued (*Rosh Hashanah*, p 11a) about whether the world was created in Tishrei or in Nisan; another debate ultimately about the relationship between natural and miraculous processes, material and spiritual realities. Both of these debates boil down to what you relate to as primary in creation - heaven or earth, the upper waters or the lower waters. These two famous sages represent either side of this archetypal debate. [Of course, the deepest and highest reality is transcendent and inclusive of both sides of this dichotomy; there is really only One.]

In fact, the Maharal teaches that the name Eliezer comes from the word *Ezer* / help (*Nesivos Olam*, Nesiv HaTeshuvah. Ch. 8. Maharsha, *Chidushei Halachos*, Hakdamah), and the name Yehoshua clearly comes from the word *Yeshua* / salvation. *Ozer* / helper means that someone is helping you, there is a problem and you are being helped out of that trouble. *Moshia* / savior means that someone is completely alleviating the issue itself. Thus, we see that this philosophical debate about the nature of the Creator and rain is encoded into the very names of the Rabbis themselves.

The B'nei Yissaschar, in his chapter on Cheshvan (*Chodesh Elul*, Ma'amar 1:18), discusses this idea further. He notes that Yehoshua (linguistically related to salvation) brought the Israelites into Eretz Yisrael for the first time; and that Ezra (linguistically related to *Ezer* and Eliezer) was the person who led the Jewish People back into Eretz Yisrael the second time. The first event, led by Yehoshua, was miraculous; accompanied by the walls of Jericho falling. Whereas the second event was historical, facilitated by worldly politicians and not accompanied by any overt miracles. Yehoshua represents the higher waters, which come about through Tefilah and Divine Providence. Eliezer represents the lower waters, which come about through the natural order. This debate, in addition to the others we have mentioned, essentially boils down to two questions: 1) does it all come from above or below? 2) What is the relationship between the two?

Aligning ourselves with Heaven and Earth

There is a similar Medrash, cited by the GR"A in *Aderes Eliyahu* while commenting on the pasuk quoted above, regarding the origin of the rains, "and [the rain] rose up from the earth." The *Medrash* records a debate between Rav Yochanan and Reish Lakish about whether the rains come from the *Avim Elyonim* / higher clouds, or the lower clouds. Rav Yochanan says that rain comes from the higher clouds, while Reish Lakish maintains that rain comes from the lower clouds. (The dichotomy of waters also exists within the sages Rav Yochanan and Reish Lakish. The name *Yochanan* has in it the word *Chein* / grace, Rav Yochanan thus represents the Tzadik, the 'beautiful' man (*Baba Metziya*, 84a), the higher reality, upper waters. Reish Lakish, is a Baal Teshuvah. His first name is Shimon which is a name connected to 'hiddenness'. He came from a very lowly place, to the rising of the 'lower waters')

This debate between Rav Yochanan and Reish Lakish is essentially the same argument as between Rabbi Eliezer and Rabbi Yehoshua: is rain a natural, automatic phenomenon, or is it miraculous and Providential? Does it come from below or above? Put another way we might ask, is the source of rain an impersonal system that indifferently interfaces with objective reality as a whole; or is the source of rain a Divine Presence capable of personal relationship with, and responsive to, the needs of each one of His creations?

Rain is thus the phenomenon that the sages contemplated to determine the nature of Hashem's relationship with creation. For, it was a given in their minds that rain revealed a wondrous expression of the Universal Creator behind creation; which is still the impersonal cosmic Creator of the philosophers. However, the question was whether or not rain also revealed an aspect of HaKadosh Baruch Hu that was personally involved and invested in each one of our lives as individuals. In other words, does

Hashem respond to our Tefilah? If so, then we each have a role to play in the state of the world, and a responsibility to perform that role to the best of our ability for the good of the whole.

The GR"A continues by quoting a teaching from *Pirkei d'Rabbi Eliezer* which states that the argument between Rav Yochanan and Reish Lakish can essentially be boiled down to a simple equation. "When Yisrael does the will of Hashem they get their rain from the Upper Waters, from the higher clouds, but when they do not do the will of Hashem, they get their rain from the Lower Waters, the lower clouds." In other words, when we are in alignment with Hashem, with Spirit, with the Infinite, with Transcendence, then we access the higher waters, but when we are not in alignment with the One, then we drink from the lower waters alone.

What this means is that when we, Klal Yisrael (or all of humanity for that sake), are elevating the world towards the above; when we direct our awareness upwards towards the above, then the above responds and moves towards us. When the *Tachtonim* / lower world is being *Ma'aleh l'Elyonim* / uplifted or directed towards the higher world, then the *Elyonim* / Above reciprocates and irrigates the earth below. In other words, when the lower waters are in a state of longing, in a state of yearning, then the higher waters descend. This is the ideal meta-erotic alignment between the upper and lower waters, and the upper and lower worlds, or levels of reality, in general.

When there is misalignment between these two waters, and all that they represent, then the rains come from the lower clouds, from the mechanical world of nature. This is not 'bad;' it is in fact very natural, as well as necessary for the world to exist at all. It is just not all there is. There are physical waters, Geshem, and there are spiritual waters, Matar. We need Geshem to survive on the most basic level, but we also know that the human does not survive, "on bread alone." The human is created in the Divine Image, and thus requires spiritual sustenance to feed our soul. What's more, as we discussed previously, the human is the very conduit through which spirit enters matter. It is through the human that the rains of Beriah, as the Arizal suggested, enter into the world of Asiyah.

And how exactly does a human being bring the upper waters down into the world? Through Tefilah.

The Depths are Rising

We have previously explored Rashi's comment hinting that there was no rain until there was a human being to pray for it; but there is another comment, on the exact same verse, which Rashi offers us in *Bereishis Rabbah* (14:1); "and [the rains] rose up from the earth." On this verse Rashi says, "He caused the deep to rise and filled the clouds with water to moisten the dust, and man was created."

Essentially, this means that in order to create man, Hashem caused the depths, the lower waters, to rise up and irrigate the dust. What does this mean? *Adam* / Man is created from *Adamah* / earth or clay, but *Afar* / dust needs moisture to form clay. Thus, for man you need clay, and for clay you need water. If it didn't rain before man was created, how then did Hashem create the human being?

Rashi (quoting the Medrash) addresses this seeming contradiction and informs us that Hashem *He'ele es haTahom* / brought out the depths, the lower waters, to rise up and lubricate the earth in order to form the body of the human; this is the natural rain from the lower world of Asiyah, as discussed. Connecting this with the previous teaching of the Arizal, we can surmise that the human was thus formed from the lower waters of Asiyah, and then Davened to awaken and bring down the rain from the upper waters of Beriah.

There are thus two levels of rain, as we have noted; the natural, physical rains (lower waters), and the miraculous, Providential rains (upper waters). The impersonal system of rain, and the intimately accessible Source of rain. The body of man, and nature in general, is nourished by the lower waters; the soul of man, and the spirit of each individual creation is nourished by the upper waters. These are elicited through Davening and relationship with the Divine.

The human being is thus birthed through the natural, physical rains of the planet, and its processes. While the descent of the spiritual rains, from the upper waters, is dependent on the conscious interaction and faithful input of the human being in relationship with the Divine. Thus, we need rain, and rain also needs us. And what does rain need from us - to pray. Why?

What is Prayer?

What is *Tefillah* / prayer? Prayer is a form of lower waters rising. We utter prayer, we vaporize prayer, it has to be wet. Prayer is the release of our energy into the universe, into the world, into Hashem. That is the very definition of lower waters rising. The lower waters then stimulate the higher waters in order to give birth to blessings in the world and our lives. According to the pasuk, " ואד יעלה מן־הארץ / and [vaporized] waters will rise from the ground..." this holds true for all rain, whether from the world of Asiyah or Beriah. But how did the lower waters rise before the human was created?

There is, what we can call, *Tefillas haOlam* / the prayer of the world, 'prayer of the biosphere,' and there is *Tefillas haAdam* / the prayer of man. There is the yearning and 'calling out' of the earth, and the yearning/prayer of humanity. What does this mean?

Simply put, prayer comes from a *Makom haCheser* / a place of lacking. There is something lacking — whether it is health, wealth, sustenance, peace, clarity, or justice — and so we pray. Even the opinion of the *Ramban*, which maintains that one does not have to pray every day, still maintains that you are in fact required, according to Torah law, to Daven when you are in need of Hashem's help, salvation, guidance, or presence. Thus, even according to the *Ramban*, Tefilah is something that you technically have to do when you are in need; it is actually a Mitzvah of the Torah in such a case.

And where do we see that the world was in a state of lack? — when the world needed to create man. It was like a baby that had to be born. The earth needed the fluidity to allow for birth. The dust needed moisture to make clay to bring forth the human being. Before that, the human was formed, but it wasn't sticking, it wasn't congealing,therefore, it could not be pushed out in its full, independent manifestation. Thus, it says that Hashem caused the *Tehom* / depths to rise up in order to moisten the earth to birth the human. In other words, like so many human mothers in labor, the earth was praying for rain, for blessing, for manifestation, for new life to emerge from within.

Then there is the *Tefillas haAdam*, when the human being is in a state of lack and longs to be filled with a rain of blessings. Previously, in the context of our human prayers, we learned that with regard to remembrance of the natural rains we say *Geshem;* and with regards to requesting Providential rains we say *Matar.* Matar is thus the rains that come from the upper waters through *Tefillas haAdam.* Geshem, on the other hand, is the rain that comes from the lower waters through the prayers of the land, the *Tefillah* of the *Aretz.*

Geshem is Gashmiyus, it's the materiality of the world. When, in the second blessing of the Amidah, we acknowledge Hashem as the, "Circulator of the winds and Bringer of the Geshem / rains, the Great G-d, the Mighty, the Awe-Inspiring," we are observing and recognizing Divine qualities and expressions that are unrelated to us. This Tefilah is not about us and our desire to receive, it is about Hashem and His ability to give; it is about Hashem's *Koach* / power to bring forth life through the biospheric cycle of the rains. This section of the Amidah is part of saying *Shevach* / praises of the Creator.

In fact, the *Koach haBorei* / strength of the Creator is demonstrated precisely in the fact that *Hakadosh Baruch Hu* created a system where the "ואד יעלה מן־הארץ / [rain] rises up from the earth." In other words, the universe is created in a state of lack where the

Gashmiyus / physical dimension needs and longs to be filled with water in order to accomplish its task of manifesting life. That longing, that prayer, reaches upwards and stimulates the rains of Asiyah. That is the miracle of the natural order, whether there is human participation or not. This is the way the world was created. This is the rain of the lower waters, which are programmed from Above. This rain, Geshem, is referred to as *Mitzido* / according to Him, meaning Hashem's design of creation as a whole system.

The definition of Matar, on the other hand, is that it is *Mitzideinu* / according to us and our efforts to impact reality above and beyond its systematic nature. Matar thus describes the rains of the upper waters, which is initiated by our prayers from below. Matar is therefore, ultimately, dependent on how we want and ask for it.

These two types of rain, Geshem and Matar, and the questions they bring into focus — whether rain is *Mitzido* / because of Him or *Mitzideinu* / because of us and our relationship with Hashem — actually encapsulates the two ways we look at rain itself. Is rain a unified flow or is each raindrop distinct? Is rain solely a natural phenomenon or is it an expression of a Personal Presence responsive to our individual prayers? Should our relationship to rain be characterized by radical amazement at the *Koach haBorei* / powers of the Creator, or by direct request for the fulfillment of personal needs?

When thinking about rain, should we be more focused on the giver (Hashem) or the receiver (us)? Is rain ultimately an expression of Chesed or Gevurah? And what is the proper balance between the two?

Connecting to the Creator through Creation

Ultimately, when it comes to rain, ואד יעלה מן־הארץ, it must always arise from below.

Rain is a *Davar Gashmi* / physical thing in this world, like any other physical thing that's part of nature. But the question, and what *Chazal* are trying to get us to appreciate, is: how do we relate to the world, the physical world around us as it is? When we are talking about a spiritual object or reality, a Mitzvah or something extraordinary, there is an automatic connection with its inherent spirituality; but how do we relate to a natural, everyday occurrence like rain? And furthermore, what does that have to do with whether we are "fulfilling the desire of Hashem" or not? What actually happens when one is עושין רצונו של מקום / doing the will of the Creator, and when one is not? What is the qualitative difference in their experience of rain?

Simply, the difference in their experience is revealed in the quality of their relationship to the things that happen all around them in the natural world. It is essentially a question of what kind of dialogue you are having with the physical world. Each of us has the ability to choose how we will experience any given situation; and specifically the ways we internalize and exude experience is what further creates that given form of experience. When you are walking the earth, and the plants are growing and it's raining, and then there is drought and there's a natural cycle of events, what is your relationship to the world around you, on a physical level?

When I'm doing a mitzvah, I know I'm doing something special. When it's *Shabbos* I know its something special. When I have something that's miraculous in my life, I'm eating *Mon* / manna,

I know I'm doing something special. But when I'm not, when it's just Gashmiyus, it's a physical phenomenon in the world that's just a phenomenon, like any other phenomena — then what? How do you put yourself, as a spiritual person, as a *Yid*, as someone who wants to have a tangible connection with HaKadosh Baruch Hu at every moment, in relationship to the myriad things that are just part of the natural order of the universe? This is a question of the utmost spiritual importance. And according to the sages, the answer to it can be found in how we relate to rain. Rain is thus Hashem's litmus test, so to speak, (and ours) to get a sense of how we relate to Hashem and His creation.

This is what Chazal are telling us: when you are in alignment with the will of Hashem, you are actually being nourished by the upper waters. It is not that you are bringing different water down into the world with your prayers. It is that your entire relationship to the exact same phenomena changes. You are no longer relating to rain as just some recycled water that evaporates and falls on account of the weather. Your relationship with all rain now is that it is mamash *Mayim Elyonim.* It is not just water, it is Hashem's blessing manifest in our lives. It is from heaven. So, whether we receive rain from the lower waters or upper waters is entirely dependent on our relationship with Hashem and His world.

When we walk down the street, or do anything no matter how mundane, when we see a brick, when we see a stone, when we see anything in this natural world — we can say it's just a stone, or we can dialogue with it. We can actually see it as an 'alive' thing. We can sense that Hashem is communicating and connecting to us through this thing, that all creation is but a vessel or medium for the Creator. This is why in Hebrew, the word for 'word' and 'thing' is the same: *D'var*.

We are meant to see that every 'thing' in this world is actually a 'word' of G-d, calling for our attention and directing our awareness to the Most High. All of life is part of our living relationship with *Elokim Chayim* / the G-d of Life or Living G-d. Is the world inert and inanimate, totally separate from Hashem (Chav V'Shalom), or is the world alive and pulsing with the breath of the Creator? That is the difference between the upper and lower waters. It's all the same rain. It is simply a matter of how you relate to it.

This is what the Arizal is alluding to in his interpretation of the verse, "ואד יעלה מן־הארץ" remember, he says that the world of Asiyah did have water. It was just not water from the world of Beriah, it wasn't the raw waters, the spiritual waters. Before the human was created there was no one that had the consciousness to look at the world and say, "Whoa! This world is an amazing, stunning place and Hashem has created, and is continuing to create, this beautiful/natural universe at every moment, and THAT in itself is a miracle!"

Hashem is present in every single moment, if we would only take care to notice. That is the point of the *Mayim Elyonim* and the *Mayim Tachtonim*. It is not just to say that we have the power to create rain when we pray and act in alignment with Hashem, but that the quality of our relationship to everything in this world determines whether we are accessing the upper or lower waters. That is why the sages say that a day of rain is as great as the resurrection of the dead, or greater, or as great as the creation of the heavens and the earth, because that really is what it's all about — rain, life, birth, blessing.

For truthfully, what is *Techi'as haMeisim* / resurrection of the dead? Techi'as haMeisim, besides the cosmic event, is another way of saying that the inanimate becomes animate, the lifeless tree all of a sudden has sap and starts sprouting fruit. This is utterly miraculous, when seen in the right way! Everything is rejuvenating at every moment. We just have to open our eyes to see the constant creation and resurrection of the world that is happening at every moment. When we actively open our eyes to the awareness of life, we become participants in the active regeneration of life.

Faith and spirituality may be initially found, but are not ultimately sustained through supernatural phenomena outside of the natural system of everyday reality; mature and lasting faith and Deveikus are nurtured and expressed in the holy ways that we relate to every moment and aspect of our lives in HaKadosh Baruch Hu's wondrous creation. When we open our eyes, we are able to see the miracle of nature and experience the *Mayim Elyonim* at every moment. This is how we too, like the earth before us, and ultimately like Hashem, can bring heaven down to earth in a veritable rain of blessings.

ESSAY 2

THE RAINS OF LIFE

RAIN IS LIFE. THOSE OF US WHO LIVE IN CITIES OR spend a lot of time indoors can be disconnected from awareness of the natural world; and from the fact that was self-evident in other eras: there is no life without rain.

Rebbe Simcha Bunim, a wise Chassidic Rebbe, perceived that there were a few people living in his city whose hearts were closed and were unable to pray or study with spiritual feeling. He instructed them to go to the country and build a bungalow by the river. This was an inconvenience to the busy urbanites, but they could not refuse to comply with the instructions of their Rebbe. They went, and when they would take a break from building, they would sit down and gaze at the river flowing by. As soon as they had completed the bungalow, the Rebbe sent word, "Now you can dismantle the house and return to the city."

When you open your eyes to nature and harmonize with it — even briefly — you can come alive to a greater degree, and realize that everything is in flow. This will open you mentally, emotionally, and spiritually.

Cheshvan is the beginning of the winter rainy season. At the end of Sukkos we began to recite *Hazkarah* / mention of Hashem's power to send rain, in the second blessing of the Amidah prayer. On the Seventh of Cheshvan, people in the Land of Israel begin to recite *Sh'eilah* / prayers of 'request' for rain, in the ninth blessing of the Amidah. The *Mabul* / Great Flood began on the 17th of Cheshvan. This month gives us an opportunity to connect vividly with the flowing life-energy of rain, and open ourselves spiritually.

On the surface, rain might seem to be a mundane, natural phenomenon, but our sages and teachers reveal worlds of meaning within it. The entire tractate of *Ta'anis* grows out of a discussion of the qualities of rain. When you are intimately aware of the blessings of rain, you realize that there is a kind of *Mechayei haMeisim* / resurrection of the dead going on all the time; you realize that Hashem is present in the world, orchestrating and enlivening everything. Every drop of water that re-awakens the vegetation around you is significant. This consciousness corresponds to the *Hazkarah* / the mention of rain in the second Beracha of the Amidah prayer, which is recited within a context of declaring Hashem's praise as One who resurrects the dead.

Once you connect to the Divine flow of life by means of Hazkara, only then do you have the open-hearted appreciation that allows you to engage in *Sh'eilah* / prayerful request — specifically the request for rain in the ninth Berachah of the Amidah. If you attempt Sh'eilah without Hazkara, you have no awareness of the 'address' of the Sh'eilah. The first three Berachos of the Amidah provide us with the *Address* of our prayers: first we need an intimate recognition of the fact that Hashem is the All-Loving, All-Powerful Transcendent Creator. Then we can go on to ask the Creator to fulfil our needs and the needs of others, which includes the needs of the different forms of vegetation.

Rain is a natural phenomenon, and just like all other phenomena, it appears to manifest without regard for the existence of human beings. We do not create rain. However, when we pray for rain we actually do, in a sense. We participate in the formation and descent of rain, and we certainly create a relationship with it.

Chazal / our Sages speak about rains that come from the upper waters, and rain that comes from the lower waters. To the naked eye, there may seem to be no difference; rain is rain. But there are, in fact, subtle spiritual differences that can be observed between the rains of upper-waters and those rains sourced in lower-wates. These differences are dependent on our relationship to the rains of life — and to all of the natural world.

There Was No Adam

The verse says, " כל שיח השדה טרם יהיה בארץ וכל־עשב השדה טרם יצמח כי לא המטיר ה אלקים

על־הארץ ואדם אין לעבד את־האדמה ואד יעלה מן־הארץ והשקה את־כל־פני־

האדמה / When no shrub of the field was yet on earth and no grasses of the field had yet sprouted, because Hashem Elokim had not sent rain upon the earth and there was no man to till the soil. A flow would well up from the ground and water the whole surface of the earth" (*Bereishis*, 2:5-6). "מלמד שיצאו דשאים ועמדו על פתח קרקע עד שבא אדם הראשון ובקש עליהם רחמים וירדו גשמים וצמחו ללמדך שהקב"ה מתאוה לתפלתן של צדיקים / This teaches that the grasses emerged and stood at the opening of the ground, but they did not grow until Adam, the first man, came and prayed for mercy upon them, then the rains came, and they sprouted. And this is meant to teach you that the Holy One, Blessed be He, desires the prayers of the righteous" (*Chulin*, 60b).

Prior to the creation of the *Adam* / human being, there was no vegetation sprouting in the world. Why? Because the Adam was not yet there to pray for rain. The Arizal (*Likkutei Torah*) teaches that Bereishis 2:5, above, means there was not yet rain coming from the higher, abstract world of Beriah (potential, the world of thought) to irrigate the earth (the actual world, the world of action). *She-fa* / Divine life-force flows down from Beriah into the world of Yetzirah (the world of formation and speech) where it is formed and formatted, and finally into Asiyah where it is made concrete and actual. Without the Adam, there was no *Memutzah* / intermediary, no element of Yetzirah, between the world of Beriah and the world of Asiyah. This meant there was no connectivity between the potential and the actual. Yetzirah is the world of *Dibur* / speech, and thus human awareness (Beriah) and prayerful speech (Yetzirah) are this connectivity of Beriah to the world of Asiyah.

There was indeed rain prior to the formation of the Adam, as in verse 6, "A flow would well up from the ground and water the whole surface of the earth" — but this was rain from the ground, i.e., rain from the world of Asiyah, not from the upper realm of Beriah. If you take humanity out of the equation, there will still be rain in the world, but that rain merely comes from natural processes within Asiyah. It will not come as a response to open-hearted prayer, the conscious and expressive relationship with the Creator, which unites earth and Heaven.

Mentioning Rain & Asking for Rain

Rabbi Yehoshua says (*Ta'anis*, 2a. *Shulchan Aruch*, Orach Chayim, 114) that from the end of Sukkos we begin to *Mazkir* / recall or mention rain in our liturgy. It was established that we only begin to *Shoel* / ask for rain in Israel from the 7th of Cheshvan, so that the *Olim* / those who had ascended to Yerushalayim (for Sukkos) would have enough time to return home safely 15 days after the end of the Festival. In the words of the Mishnah, "כדי שיגיע אחרון שבישראל לנהר פרת / so that the last (pilgrim) of Israel (who traveled to Yerushalayim on foot for the Festival) can reach the Euphrates River (without being inconvenienced by rain on his journey home)" (*Ta'anis*, 10a). In *Bavel* / Babylon, they began to ask for rain on the 60th day of the season (ובגולה עד ששים בתקופה). Rashi (ibid) writes that the whole world, besides the Land of Israel, follows Bavel in this regard. The Rosh argues (see *Tur*, Orach Chayim, 117), that we should all ask for rain whenever we need it, but the Halachah is according to Rashi.

During the Amidah we mention rain twice; in the second blessing we are Mazkir rain, and in the ninth blessing we are Shoel rain. The 'mention' of rain in the second blessing of the Amidah corresponds to the element of *Shevach* or *Tehilah* / praise, while the 'request' for rain in the ninth blessing corresponds to the element of *Tefilah* / prayer (*Rashi, Tosefos*, Berachos, 29a. See *Ohr Sameach*, Rambam, Hilchos Tefilah, 10:8).

There are many different words for rain in the Torah: Geshem and Matar, *Yoreh* / early rains and *Malkosh* / late rains. The two kinds of rain mentioned in the Amidah are Geshem and Matar. In the second blessing, the *Hazkarah* / mention is of Geshem. In the ninth blessing the *Sh'eilah* is for Matar. What is the difference between these kinds of rain? So far we can map the following details:

Geshem	'Mentioned' in the preliminary praises of the Amidah	Inserted in Amidah during the end of Sukkos	Descends from the lower world of Asiyah, as a natural phenomenon	Does not necessarily give life to vegetation; creates 'clay'
Matar	'Requested' in the middle prayers of the Amidah	Inserted in the Amidah during Cheshvan and later	Descends from the higher world of Beriah, in response to human prayer	Gives life to vegetation

Geshem & Matar

Rabbeinu Bachya writes (*Devarim*, 11:17), that Geshem comes from the rising of the earth's vapor or mist, which rises to the sky, becomes clouds, and then rains down. *Geshem* comes from the word *Gashmi* / physicality; מלשון גשמות ודבר גופני / from the language of something physical and coarse. Geshem is from below, the lower waters; it is a natural phenomenon (as the Malbim explains) created by Hashem.

Geshem is the way *Shefa* / flow, or *Chomer* / the pure potential of rain, becomes manifest in *Tzurah* / physical form. With Geshem there is a 'natural' *Chibur* / connecting of Heaven and earth: the mist below rises above, and then it becomes manifest as Geshem below. Thus we 'mention' that Hashem is *Morid haGeshem* / the One Who makes the Geshem descend — by making mist ascend from below.

Chazal tell us (*Ta'anis*, 7b), "גדול יום הגשמים כיום שנבראו שמים וארץ / The day of the Geshamim is as great as the day on which *Shamayim v'haAretz* / the Heavens and earth were created." This again suggests that Geshem is the unity between Heaven and earth. Heaven is *Bli Tzurah* / without defined form; it is like an undifferentiated mass or unit. The word שמים /*Shamayim* alludes to the phrase שם מים / *Sham Mayim* / water is there, as in water without form. The term *Geshem* means a downpour. When water pours down onto the earth and saturates the *Afar* / dust, it becomes *Aretz* / land, from the word *Ratz* / running, moving, growing. The multiplicity of dust particles blend as one, and enter a state of flow, to become as an undifferentiated mass of clay. Then the Oneness Above is mirrored in a oneness below.

Matar, on the other hand, is related to the word *meter* in English — it's a 'measured' sprinkling of rain given in proportion to precise needs. Matar consists of individual raindrops that fall to earth, allowing the particles of Afar to maintain their individuality as well. Matar comes from Above, that is, it comes from *Hashgachah* / Divine providence, rather than from *Teva* / nature (*Malbim*).

Higher Waters & Lower Waters

Rabbi Eliezer says, "כל העולם כולו ממימי אוקיינוס הוא שותה / the entire world receives water from the waters of *Okyanus* / the lower
waters i.e., the ocean." Rabbi Yehoshua says, "כל העולם כולו ממים
העליונים הוא שותה / all the world receives water from the Upper Waters (*Ta'anis*, 9b).

Rabbi Eliezer and Rabbi Yehoshua also debate when the world
was created — actually referring to the day that humanity was created (*Rosh Hashanah*, p 11a). R. Eliezer's opinion is that it was on the
first day of the month of Tishrei, Rosh Hashanah, meaning within
the context of 'below.' R. Yehoshua, however, asserts that it was on
the first day of the month of Nissan, the month of transcendent
miracles, meaning within the context of 'Above.'

The names of Rabbi Eliezer and Rabbi Yehoshua also allude
to these different perspectives. The Maharal (*Nesivos Olam*, Nesiv
HaTeshuvah. Ch. 8) as well as the Maharsha (*Chidushei Halachos*,
Hakdamah), explain that the meaning of the name *Eliezer* is *E-l
Ezer* / Hashem helps; and the name *Yehoshua* means, "Hashem will
bring you a salvation."

Both of their names are related to help/salvation. However, 'help'
implies that something is wrong and yet there is assistance. The
situation may not change, but someone is there to help. 'Salvation'
means, the help is so successful or profound that there is no longer any problem. Yehoshua thus represents a level that is higher
than Eliezer, alluding to the upper waters, the world created in the
month of Nisan, and the idea of Matar.

To further support this, Yehoshua led Klal Yisrael into the Holy Land for the first time in our history. This was a time of miracles, including the fall of Jericho, and the day the sun stood still. Ezra, on the other hand, led the Jews back to the Holy Land after the First Exile. They were allowed to return to Israel because King Darius gave them permission; it was a 'natural' event (*Bnei Yissaschar*, Chodesh Elul, Ma'amar 1:18).

This same dichotomy exists between the sages Rav Yochanan and Reish Lakish. The name *Yochanan* has in it the word *Chein* / grace, as explored earlier. Rav Yochanan thus represents the Tzadik, the 'beautiful' man (*Baba Metziya*), the higher reality. Reish Lakish, on the other hand, is a Baal Teshuvah (His first name is Shimon which is a name connected to 'hiddenness). He came from a very low place, 'below.'

The Medrash says (*Bereishis Rabbah*. See the Gra, *Aderes Eliyahu*, on the Pasuk *V'eid Yaalu*), Rav Yochanan's opinion is that rain comes from 'clouds' Above, and Reish Lakish's opinion is that rain comes from 'clouds' below. Pirkei d'Rebbe Eliezer reconciles these opinions, "When Yisrael does the will of Hashem, they get their rain from the Upper Waters; but when they do not do the will of Hashem, they get their rain from the Lower Waters."

The Prayers of Nature & the Prayers of Humanity

Prayer, by definition, is based in חסר / *Cheser* / lack. The mist rising from the ground represents Tefilah — either human Tefilah, or a Tefilah which is the natural yearning for fulfilment of the earth itself. When the earth is parched, it yearns for the Gashmiyus of rain, its mist rises and rain comes down on Hashem's terms. When we are parched, our prayers of yearning are the mists that rise to Hashem, and rain descends on our terms. The moisture of our mouth rises and arouses the waters from Above to descend in the form of a Divine kiss.

We naturally associate a downpour with tears. The teardrops that descend upon us from Above (in response to our prayers) are like tears of longing Tefilah. Water represents Chesed. It is as if our Supernal Beloved is weeping and yearning for us, praying that we receive His intimate Chesed. Rain is likened to the Divine 'semen' which impregnates the earth and all of life below, "מיטרא בעלה דארעא / rain is the husband of the earth" (*Ta'anis*, 6b. See also, Yerushalmi, *Berachos*, 9:2).

All rain comes as an 'arousal' from below, a 'prayer' from the lower reality. This is the way of the world, the realm of natural causality. In nature there is a system, a recycling of life; the moisture of life below rises, is retained above, and is redistributed in some manner. This is the naturally-occurring "prayer of the biosphere." According to the natural-order of causality, however, the clouds are passively carried wherever the wind blows — perhaps even far out to sea. This is in contrast to the prayer of the human being. When we *Daven*/pray and send our energy Above, not only do we stimulate the downflow, we unite with the Distributor, our 'Husband,' the Giver beyond natural causality. We also make vessels so that we can receive rain as Chesed in the form of blessings, and not as Gevurah in the form of a 'curse' or flood, Heaven forbid.

The rainwater is the same in both cases, the difference is in how we relate to its Source. Are we active participants or mere passive recipients? Are we releasing the spiritual 'mist' of our mouths through prayer to stimulate rain from Heaven; or is there just a natural process of physical moisture rising to stimulate rain from the clouds?

When we produce 'rain' through our prayers, we make ourselves into the vessel for blessings. When we turn to face the Source of Blessing instead of turning away to face the interplay of natural forces, we open ourselves to receive from the Source. The Rokeach (Rabbi Eliezer of Worms), in *Hilchos Sukkos* (Hoshanah Rabbah), speaks of how the words of our prayers are like rain; " ויחלו כמטר לי ופיהם פערו למלקוש / *U-Fihem Pa'aru l'Malkosh* / For the late rains, their mouths open wide" (*Iyov*, 29:23). The mention of "mouths" in this verse alludes to prayer. Through prayer we make ourselves a vessel for what we want and wish to receive.

Hazkarah & Sh'eilah, Revisited

The Hazkarah of Geshem is within the blessing of *Techiyas haMeisim* / resurrection of the dead. The Gemara (*Ta'anis*, 7a) says this is because *Geshamim* / rains are *Gadol* / great like *Techiyas haMeisim*. Furthermore, "גדול יום הגשמים מתחיית המתים / The day of rain is greater than the resurrection of the dead." The Yerushalmi (also beginning of Ta'anis) says, "כשם שתחיית המתים חיים לעולם כך ירידת גשמים חיים לעולם / Just as *Techiyas haMeisim* brings *Chai l'Olam* / life to the world, so does rain… like the day the world was created."

Techiyas haMeisim, along with the second blessing of the Amidah, express the quality of Gevurah (The second blessing begins with אתה גיבור / You are Powerful (Gevurah), it corresponds to Yitzchak). Water is Chesed, yet it comes down to the world joined together with the Sefira of Gevurah, as a Yichud between both these Midos (*Zohar* 2, 154b. *Zohar* 3, 32a).

Hazkarah expresses the *Shevach* / praise of Hashem. In praise there is no place for human differences, as there is no receiver implied. It's all about the Giver, "*Atah Gibor l'Olam Hashem / You* are Powerful forever, Hashem." In terms of the Hazakara of Geshem, it is not about our varying needs for rain; it's about the uniform qualities of the Creator that are involved in making rain appear. We mention Geshem as the *Gashmiyus* / physicality of Rain, "Hashem, you are so *Gibor* / powerful that You can make Yourself present even in the dense physicality of falling rain!" Since in the Shevach of Hashem, there are no distinctions, everyone in the world starts the Hazkarah of Geshem on the same date. This is part of the *Mitzvah* of *Lo Sisgodedu* / do not splinter the world community into factions.*

---

* *Lo Sisgodedu* is expressed in our tradition to begin the Hazkarah of Geshem in the Musaf service of Shemini Atzeres. It would be logical to start the Hazkara at the beginning of Shemini Atzeres — at Ma'ariv. However, our Sages were concerned that it was sometimes dangerous to attend a public Ma'ariv service, and therefore not everyone would be able to attend that service. Some might then begin Hazkara in Ma'ariv and others in Shacharis the next morning, creating different practices. In addition, others might arrive to Shul late in the morning, and begin Hazkara in Musaf. Since in general the whole community would be able to gather for Musaf, this became the obvious choice for a unified beginning of Hazkara. See *Yevamos*, 13b-14a. *Shulchan Aruch*, Orach Chayim, 114.

When we are asking for rain, we use the term *Matar*. Drops of Matar come because of the prayers of individuals, " מטר בשביל יחיד / Matar / Rain is for the *Yachid* / individual" (*Ta'anis* 9a-b, the opinion of both Rav Yochanan and Reish Lakish). There are *Chilukim* / distinctions present, and thus different individuals start the Sh'eilah on different dates. In the Land of Israel the prayer starts on the Seventh of Cheshvan; in the Diaspora, 60 days after the beginning of solar autumn.

With this in mind, we can understand the Tefilah of the Kohen Gadol, that Hashem should not listen to the *Perat* / individual supplicant, at the expense of the *Klal* / collective or majority of the People; 'If a person traveling prays that it should not rain, don't listen to his prayer, because the Klal needs rain!'

Even though Matar descends because of the needs of individuals (and is aroused by means of individual's Tefilah), still, the Kohen Gadol is asking that the rain should come because of the Klal. This places the individual into the context of the Klal.

Since Geshem comes not through human participation, but rather, through the general will of the Creator, Geshem is on Hashem's terms, so-to-speak. Geshem is rooted in the infinite, non-variable *Chesed* / giving, the undifferentiated *Tovah* / beneficence. A lot of rain is called *Rov Tovah* / a lot of good (*Ta'anis*, 23a).

Matar is a 'higher' and 'deeper' form of rain that comes from the *Peratim* / details of our distinct needs, as well as Gevurah. The Gemara (*Baba Basra*, 16a) says that Hashem told Iyov, "הרבה טיפין / בראתי בעבים וכל טיפה וטיפה בראתי לה דפוס בפני עצמה / Many drops I have created in the clouds, and each and every drop I have created from a unique and singular mold." This is the dimension of rain that relates to distinct individuals. However, like the Kohen, we want the Matar to be not just on our terms, but on the Infinite One's terms. We want the *Shefa* / downflow, even upon diverse individuals, to be rooted in The ever-constant Kindness. We want even the Gevurah of rain, the individual droplets, to be delivered in a way of Chesed. This combination of Gevurah and Chesed is called *Rachamim* / mercy — and *Gishmei Berachah* / rains of blessing.

To elicit this, to the best of our ability, we pray for Matar as a *Klal* / whole, and thus connect to the *Klal Gadol* / greater collective. Although we ask according to our specific needs, along with the distinct needs of the land in which we reside, we unify the beginning of our Davening for Matar to the greatest extent possible. That is, if we are anywhere in the world outside of Eretz Yisrael, we begin the Tefilah according to the Babylonian date. When we are thus *Mechubar* / connected to the Klal, the rain that descends has more of the element of Infinite *Chesed* / loving-kindness of Hashem.

Thus our prayerful requests for the nourishment of rain are not simply for the sake of human, finite, needs; nor rain "on our terms." Rather, we concern ourselves with how all individuals, with all of their different needs, are embraced within the Klal of Yisrael. When our prayers are *b'Sheim Kol Yisrael* / in the name of all the individuals of Israel, it is as if we are praying as one Klal; and we can thus connect powerfully with Hashem, the Infinite One.

Rains of Revelation

From the Geshem of Asiyah that fell prior to the creation of Adam — the "flow that welled up from the ground" — clay was made. This was the very clay with which Hashem created the human being. But what is the purpose of our creation?

Our purpose and work as human beings is to consciously 'connect' heaven and earth. When we do this, rain descends from Above (*Aderes Eliyahu* on the Pasuk, "v'Eid Ya'alu"). Through our Davening and actions below, we touch Hashem, and this creates a conduit through which water descends from Heaven in proportion to our needs.

Rashi writes that in order to create Adam, Hashem elevated the *Tehom* / depths, which irrigated the clouds so they should rain, and make the earth wet. Then the shape of Adam was formed from the resulting clay. "He caused the deep to rise and filled the clouds with water to moisten the dust, and man was created" (*Rashi*, Bereishis, 2:6. *Medrash Rabbah*, Bereishis, 14:1). Thus we see two movements: a) to create Adam rain was needed, and b) since the creation of Adam, rain is dependent on the prayers of humanity. Thus, we were created by means of rain, and we were created so that we would pray and bring rain. Creation needs us in order to sprout and flourish, because we need Creation to sprout and flourish.

Davening for rain not only attunes us to the rhythms of Creation, it attunes us to our relationship with the Creator. In this intimate relationship, we reveal our presence through prayer and Hashem reveals the Divine Presence through the rain fall.

Thus the Creator of nature is one with nature; all is one grand, multidirectional flow of Divine Life.

Rain is a *Mashal* / parable for life in this world. Is your experience of life one of Geshem, a mass of Gashmiyus, Lower Waters? Or is your experience of life as is Matar, with every single Perat uniquely formed by Divine Intelligence and Love? Can you sense the Infinite Ocean of Kindness in a single physical drop of water?

Other Books by the Author

RECLAIMING THE SELF
The Way of Teshuvah

Teshuvah is one of the great gifts of life. It speaks of a hope for a better today and empowers us to choose a brighter tomorrow. But what exactly is Teshuvah? How does it work? How can we undo our past and how do we deal with guilt? And what is healthy regret without eroding our self-esteem? In this fascinating and empowering book, the path for genuine transformation and a way to include all of our past in the powerful moment of the now, is explored and demonstrated.

THE MYSTERY OF KADDISH
Understanding the Mourner's Kaddish

The Mystery of Kaddish is an in-depth exploration into the Mourner's Prayer. Throughout Jewish history, there have been many rites and rituals associated with loss and mourning, yet none have prevailed quite like the Mourner's Kaddish Prayer, which has become the definitive ritual of mourning. The book explores the source of this prayer and deconstructs the meaning to better understand the grieving process and how the Kaddish prayer supports and uplifts the bereaved through their own personal journey to healing.

UPSHERNISH: The First Haircut
Exploring the Laws, Customs & Meanings
of a Boy's First Haircut

What is the meaning of Upsherin, the traditional celebration of a boy's first haircut at the age of three? Why is a boy's hair allowed to grow freely for his first three years? What is the deeper import of hair in all its lengths and varieties? What is the meaning of hair coverings? Includes a guide to conducting an Upsherin ceremony.

A BOND FOR ETERNITY
Understanding the Bris Milah

What is the Bris Milah – the covenant of circumcision? What does it represent, symbolize and signify? This book provides an in depth and sensitive review of this fundamental Mitzvah. In this little masterpiece of wisdom – profound yet accessible —the deeper meaning of this essential rite of passage and its eternal link to the Jewish people, is revealed and explored.

REINCARNATION AND JUDAISM
The Journey of the Soul

A fascinating analysis of the concept of Gilgul / Reincarnation. Dipping into the fountain of ancient wisdom and modern understanding, this book addresses and answers such basic questions as: What is reincarnation? Why does it occur? And how does it affect us personally?

INNER RHYTHMS
The Kabbalah of MUSIC

Exploring the inner dimension of sound and music, and particularly, how music permeates all aspects of life. The topics range from Deveikus/Unity and Yichudim/Unifications, to the more personal issues, such as Simcha/Happiness and Marirus/ sadness.

MEDITATION AND JUDAISM
Exploring the Jewish Meditative Paths

A comprehensive work encompassing the entire spectrum of Jewish thought, from the sages of the Talmud and the early Kabbalists to the modern philosophers and Chassidic masters. This book is both a scholarly, in-depth study of meditative practices, and a practical, easy to follow guide for any person interested in meditating the Jewish way.

TOWARD THE INFINITE

A book focusing exclusively on the Chassidic approach to meditation known as Hisbonenus. Encompassing the entire meditative experience, it takes the reader on a comprehensive and engaging journey through this unique practice. The book explores the various states of consciousness that a person encounters in the course of the meditation, beginning at a level of extreme self-awareness and concluding with a state of total non-awareness.

THIRTY – TWO GATES OF WISDOM
into the Heart of Kabbalah & Chassidus

What is Kabbalah? And what are the differences between the theoretical, meditative, magical and personal Kabbalistic teachings? What are the four paths of interpreting the teachings of the ARIzal? What did Chassidus teach? These are some of the fundamental issues expanded upon in this text. And then, more specifically, why are there so many names of G-d and what do they represent? What are the key concepts of these deeper teachings?

The book explores the grand narrative of the great chain of reality, how there was and is a movement from the Infinite Oneness of Hashem to a world of (apparent) duality and multiplicity.

THE PURIM READER
The Holiday of Purim Explored

With a Persian name, a masquerade dress code and a woman as the heroine, Purim is certainly unusual amongst the Jewish holidays. Most people are very familiar with the costumes, Megilah and revelry, but are mystified by their significance. This book offers a glimpse into the hidden world of Purim, uncovering these mysteries and offering a deeper understanding of this unique holiday.

EIGHT LIGHTS
8 Meditations for Chanukah

What is the meaning and message of Chanukah? What is the spiritual significance of the Lights of the Menorah? What are the Lights telling us? What is the deeper dimension of the Dreidel? Rav Pinson, with his trademark deep learning and spiritual sensitivity guides us through eight meditations relating to the Lights of the Menorah, the eight days of Chanukah, and a fascinating exploration of the symbolism and structure of the Dreidel. Includes a detailed how-to guide for lighting the Chanukah Menorah.

THE IYYUN HAGADAH
An Introduction to the Haggadah

In this beautifully written introduction to Passover and the Haggadah, we are guided through the major themes of Passover and the Seder night. This slim text, addresses the important questions, such as: What is the big deal of Chametz? What are we trying to achieve through conducting a Seder? What's with all that stuff on the Seder Plate? And most importantly, how is this all related to freedom?

PASSPORT TO KABBALAH
A Journey of Inner Transformation

Life is a journey full of ups and downs, inside-outs, and unexpected detours. There are times when we think we know exactly where we want to be headed, and other times when we are so lost we don't even know where we are. This slim book provides readers with a passport of sorts to help them through any obstacles along their path of self-refinement, reflection, and self-transformation.

———

THE FOUR SPECIES
The Symbolism of the Lulav & Esrog

The Four Species have inspired countless commentaries and traditions and intrigued scholars and mystics alike. In this little masterpiece of wisdom both profound and practical - the deep symbolic roots and nature of the Four Species are explored. The Na'anuim, or ritual of the Lulav movement, is meticulously detailed and Kavanos,, are offered for use with the practice. Includes an illustrated guide to the Lulav Movements.

———

THE BOOK OF LIFE AFTER LIFE

What is a soul? What happens to us after we physically die?

What is consciousness, and can it survive without a physical brain?

Can we remember our past lives?

Do near-death experiences prove immortality?

What is Gan Eden? Resurrection?

Exploring the possibility of surviving death, the near-death experience and a glimpse into what awaits us after this life.

(This book is an updated and expanded version of the book; Jewish Wisdom of the Afterlife)

THE GARDEN OF PARADOX:
The Essence of Non - Dual Kabbalah

This book is a Primer on the Essential Philosophy of Kabbalah presented as a series of 3 conversations, revealing the mysteries of Creator, Creation and Consciousness. With three representational students, embodying respectively, the philosopher, the activist and the mystic, the book, tackles the larger questions of life. Who is G-d? Who am I? Why do I exist? What is my purpose in this life? Written in clear and concise prose, the text, gently guides the reader towards making sense of life's paradoxes and living meaningfully.

BREATHING & QUIETING THE MIND

Achieving a sense of self-mastery and inner freedom demands that we gain a measure of hegemony over our thoughts. We learn to choose out thoughts so that we are not at the mercy of whatever belches up to the mind. Through quieting the mind and conscious breathing we can slow the onrush of anxious, scattered thinking and come to a deeper awareness of the interconnectedness of all of life.

Source texts are included in translation, with how-to-guides for the various practices.

VISUALIZATION AND IMAGERY:
Harnessing the Power of our Mind's Eye

We assume that what we see with our eyes is absolute. Yet, beyond our ability to choose what we see, we have the ability to choose how we see. This directly translates into how we experience life. In a world saturated with visual imagery, our senses are continuously assaulted with Kelipa/empty/fantasy imagery that we would not necessarily choose. These images can negatively affect our relationship with ourselves, with the world around us, and with the Divine. This volume seeks to show us how we can alter that which we observe through harnessing the power of our mind's eye, the inner sanctum of our imagination. We thus create a new way to see and experience the world. This book teaches us how to utilize visualization and imagery as a way to develop our spiritual sensitivity and higher intuition, and ultimately achieve Deveikus/Unity with Hashem.

SOUND AND VIBRATION:
Tuning into the Echoes of Creation

Through our perception of sound and vibration we internalize the world around us. What we hear, and how we process that hearing, has a profound impact on how we experience life. What we hear can empower us or harm us. A defining human capacity is to harness the power sound -- through speech, dialogue, and song, and through listening to others. Hearing is primary dimension of our existence. In fact, as a fetus our ears were the first fully operating sensory organs to develop.

This book will guide you in methods of utilizing the power of sound and vibration to heal and maintain mental, emotional and spiritual health, to fine-tune your Midos and even to guide you into deeper levels of Deveikus / conscious unity with Hashem. The vibratory patterns of the Aleph-Beis are particularly useful portals into our deeper conscious selves. Through chanting and deep listening, we can use the letters and sounds to shift our very mindset, to induce us into a state of presence and spiritual elevation.

THE POWER OF CHOICE:
A Practical Guide to Conscious Living

It is the essential premise of this book that we hold the key to unlock many of the gates that seem closed to us and keep us from living our fullest life. That key we all hold is the power to choose. The Power of Choice is the primary tool that we have at our disposal to impact the world and effect change within our own lives. We often give up this power to outside forces such as the market, media, politicians or peer pressure; or to internal forces that often function beyond our conscious control such as ego, anger, lust, greed or jealousy. Making conscious, compassionate and creative decisions is the cornerstone of living a mature and meaningful life.

MYSTIC TALES FROM THE EMEK HAMELECH

Mystic Tales of the Emek HaMelech, is a wondrous and inspiring collection of stories culled from the Emek HaMelech. Emek HaMelech, from which these stories have been taken, (as well as its author) is a bit of a mystery. But like all good mysteries, it is one worth investigating. In this spirit the present volume is being offered to the general public in the merit and memory of its saintly author, as well as in the hopes of introducing a vital voice of deeper Torah teaching and tradition to a contemporary English speaking audience

---

INNER WORLDS OF JEWISH PRAYER
A Guide to Develop and Deepen the Prayer Experience

While much attention has been paid to the poetry, history, theology and contextual meaning of the prayers, the intention of this work is to provide a guide to finding meaning and effecting transformation through the prayer experience itself.

Explore: *What happens when we pray? *How do we enter the mind-state of prayer? *Learning to incorporate the body into the prayers. *Discover techniques to enhance and deepen prayer and make it a transformative experience.

This empowering and inspiring text, demonstrates how through proper mindset, preparation and dedication, the experience of prayer can be deeply transformative and ultimately, life-altering.

WRAPPED IN MAJESTY
Tefillin - Exploring the Mystery

Tefillin, the black boxes and leather straps that are worn during prayer, are curiously powerful and mysterious. Within the inky black boxes lie untold secrets. In this profound, passionate and thought-provoking text, the multi-dimensional perspectives of Tefillin are explored and revealed. Magically weaving together all levels of Torah including the Peshat (literal observation), to Remez (allegorical), to Derush, (homiletic), to Sod (hidden) into one beautiful tapestry. Inspirational and instructive, Wrapped in Majesty: Tefillin, will make putting on the Tefillin more meaningful and inspiring.

SECRETS OF THE MIKVAH:
Waters of Transformation

A Mikvah is a pool of water used for the purpose of ritual immersion; a place where one moves from a state of Tumah; impurity, blockage and death—to a place of Teharah; purity, fluidity and life.

In SECRETS OF THE MIKVAH, Rav Pinson delves into the transformative powers of the Mikvah with his trademark all-encompassing perspective that ranges from the literal, Pshat observation and Halachic implications of the texts, to the allegorical, the philosophical, and finally, to the deep secrets of the

Mikvah as revealed by Kabbalah and Chassidus.

This insightful and inspirational text demonstrates how immersion in a Mikvah can be a transformative and life-altering practice, and includes various Kavanos—deep intentions—for all people, through various stages of life, that empower and enrich the immersion experience.

———————

THE SPIRAL OF TIME:
A 12 Part Series on the Months of the Year.
The following titles from the series are now available!

THE SPIRAL OF TIME:
Unraveling the Yearly Cycle

Many centuries ago, the Sages of Israel were the foremost authority in the fields of both astronomical calculation and astrological wisdom, including the deeper interpretations of the cycles and seasons. Over time, this wisdom became hidden within the esoteric teachings of the Torah, and as a result was known only to students and scholars of the deepest depths of the tradition. More recently, the great teachers, from R. Yitzchak Luria (the Arizal) to the Baal Shem Tov, taught that as the world approaches the Era of Redemption, it is a Mitzvah / spiritual obligation to broadly reveal this wisdom.

"The Spiral of Time" is volume 1 is a series of 12 books, and serves as an introductory book to the basic concepts and nature of the Hebrew calendar and explores the special day of Rosh Chodesh.

———————

THE MONTH OF SHEVAT:
ELEVATING EATING
& The Holiday of Tu b'Shevat

Each month of the year radiates with a distinct Divine energy and thus unique opportunities for growth, *Tikkun* and illumination. According to the deeper teachings of the Torah, all of these distinct qualities, opportunities and natural phenomena correspond to a certain data set. That is, the nature of each month is elucidated by a specific letter of the Aleph Beis, a tribe, verse, human sense, and so forth. The month of Shevat is particularly connected to food and our relationship to bodily intake. During this month we celebrate Tu b'Shevat, the New Year of the Tree, and aspire to create a proper and physically/emotionally/spiritually healthy relationship with food.

THE MONTH OF IYYAR: EVOLVING THE SELF
& The Holiday of LAG B'OMER

The month of IYYAR is the second month of the spring, a month that connects the Redemption from Egypt in Nissan with the Revelation of Torah in Sivan. The Chai/ Eighteenth day of the Month is the day we celebrate the Rashbi (Rabbi Shimon Bar Yochai) and the revealing of the hidden aspects of the Torah. This is the 'Holiday' of Lag b'Omer. The book explores the unique quality of this special month, a month that has a Mitzvah of counting the Omer every day. In addition, the book explores the roots and significance of the mystical 'holiday' of Lag b'Omer. Including the customs & Practices of Lag b'Omer, such as, bonfires, bows & arrows, parades, Upsherin, and more.

THE MONTHS OF TAMUZ AND AV:
Embracing Brokenness -
17th of Tamuz, Tisha B'Av, & Tu B'Av

Each month and season of the year, radiates with distinct Divine qualities and unique opportunities for growth and Tikkun.

The summer month of Tamuz and Av contain the longest and hottest days of the year. The raised temperature is indicative of a corresponding spiritual heat, a time of harsher judgement and potential destruction, such as the destructions of the first and second Beis HaMikdash, which began on the 17th of Tamuz and culminated on the 9th and 10th of Av.

A few days later, on Tu b'Av, the darkness is transformed and reveals the greatest light and possibility for new life. During these summer months of Tamuz and Av we embrace our brokenness so that we can heal and transform darkness into light.

THE MONTH OF ELUL:
Days of Introspection and Transformation

Each month of the year radiates with a distinct quality and provides unique opportunities for growth and personal transformation. Elul, as the final month of the spring/summer season is connected to endings. Elul gives us the strength to be able to finish strong, to end well. Elul also serves as a month of preparation for the New Year/Rosh Hashanah.

We inhale our past year, ending with wisdom and then we also gain the wisdom to begin anew and exhale a positive year into being. The mental, emotional, and spiritual objective of this month is introspection and the reclaiming of our inner purity and wholeness.

THE MONTH OF TEVES:
Refining Relationships, Elevating the Body

The quality of Teves is generally harsh—much like its counterpart Tamuz in the summer, thus the tendency for many is to hunker down, retract, curl up and wait for the month to pass by, only to reemerge when the harshness has dissipated. Think for a moment about the 'easier' months of the year, which, like gentle waves in the ocean, carry us where we want to go. We can ride these energies easily and they can propel us forward effortlessly, we just need to go with the overall flow, so to speak. The harsher months, on the other hand, can be compared to the more powerful waves that emanate from the belly of the ocean,which come forcefully crashing down and can easily drown a person before they even realize what has happened. However, those who want to utilize the momentum of the powerful energy that is available during such times can, with caution and creativity, harness these intense waves and ride them higher and farther than other, more gentle circumstances may allow. However, harnessing the power of Tohu, the raw energy of the body, does in fact need to be approached with great care and attention.
